P9-AQT-660

Island at the Center of the World

ISLAND
AT THE CENTER
OF THE WORLD

New Light on Easter Island

BY FATHER SEBASTIAN ENGLERT

Translated and Edited by William Mulloy
Photographs by George Holton

Charles Scribner's Sons · New York

Titlepage: Moai on the flank
of the statue quarry
at Rano Raraku as seen at sunset

Father Sebastian Englert
with a modern version of the
traditional wooden statues
called moai kavakava

↪CONTENTS

⌒ ILLUSTRATIONS

◄ FOREWORD

by William Mulloy

Professor of Anthropology
University of Wyoming

FOR NEARLY THIRTY-FIVE YEARS FATHER SEBASTIAN ENGLERT WAS THE PARISH
priest on Easter Island, a tiny mote of land located in the South Pacific
about 2300 miles west of the coast of South America. His lot was to
serve the religious needs of the more than 1400 members of one
of the more isolated communities of the world and he thus spent a
great part of his life in Hangaroa, the island's one village, with
only the rarest of opportunities to see any other part of the world.
Throughout most of his tenure, ships dropped anchor at Easter Island
only about once or twice each year. Though his religious duties were
strenuous and time-consuming and until shortly before his death he
had to carry them out alone, he was more than a dedicated priest. He
found time to be an active culture historian and linguist as well. Under conditions of isolation from professional colleagues and with limited library resources that would have discouraged most students at
the outset, he remained a systematic investigator of the island, its language, its people, and their history and prehistory. Indeed his works
developed a special kind of value because of the extreme isolation
in which he studied. Lack of contact with colleagues had at least the
virtue of preventing him from being influenced by the orientations
and preconceptions of others. Extreme poverty of library resources
served a similar purpose, while at the same time forcing him to devote

9

his attention primarily to the objective facts he could collect on the island. Thus his work is uniquely independent, and herein perhaps lies a great part of its significance. He had intimate contact with the island's people, developed greater fluency in the local language than any other outsider, and profited by penetrating local insights far beyond the capacity of other investigators. Most important of all is the fact that he loved the island and its people, and this emotion was returned in equal measure by the islanders. No other investigator has ever been able to achieve a similar intensity of rapport.

His most extensive work about the island, though by no means his only one, is *La Tierra de Hotu Matu'a*, published in Santiago, Chile, in 1948. It is an excellent and detailed summary of the history, archaeology, ethnology, and language of the island and has been widely used and quoted by students of the Pacific. A new edition of this book with extensive additions based on recent research is currently in press. The linguistic material has been greatly increased and will form a separate volume. It is an exhaustive presentation, and the only one we have, of all that has survived of the earlier form of the language. The last section of this voluminous, handwritten manuscript was delivered to the publisher less than a month before the author's death.

Father Sebastian was born in the town of Dillingen an der Donau in Bavaria on November 17, 1888. He was educated at Eichstätt and Burghausen. In 1907 he entered the Capuchin Order of Franciscan Friars and studied philosophy and theology in Dillingen. He was ordained a priest in 1912. From 1917 until the end of the First World War he served as a chaplain in the German Army in France and Belgium. At the war's end he was appointed to a Capuchin parish in Munich. In 1922, at his own request, he was sent to Chile as a missionary to the Araucanian Indians, serving in Villa Rica and Pucón. Here too he supplemented his service to his congregation with ethnological and linguistic research and published several works. In

1935 he volunteered to serve in the missionary parish on Easter Island and remained there for the rest of his life.

When I came to the island in 1955 as a member of an archaeological expedition led by the Norwegian explorer and investigator Thor Heyerdahl, this remarkable man was the first person I encountered when I stepped ashore at Hotu Iti. While he made me welcome I was immediately impressed with his pride in the island and the sincerity with which he expressed it, as well as the profound respect and affection manifested by the group of islanders that surrounded him. In the first ten minutes of our contact it was apparent that here was someone unusual, and I became anxious to learn what manner of man he was. The months and years that followed gave ample opportunity.

Very shortly after the expedition's arrival he was asked to summarize the results of his own researches into the island's history and prehistory for the visiting archaeologists. I well remember the diffidence and the humility with which he approached the task, and his feeling, which he made known to me, that it was not quite fitting for him to express his own opinions before a group of professional scholars. He did not reveal that he was aware that these same archaeologists were prepared for the work ahead only by having read a welter of frustrating literature, much of which was contradictory, incomplete, and in some cases downright incorrect. We were facing the unknown, and each of us was trying desperately to develop some kind of orientation with which to begin the investigations that lay ahead. Father Sebastian gave us a magnificent lecture based largely on ideas he had developed from his analysis of the local traditions. I for one found myself hastily writing down a great many things that I didn't even understand, some of which I understood only after years had passed. I still have those notes, and they continue to be useful.

Without Father Sebastian's subsequent aid, our work would not have been succesful. He helped us to obtain archaeological workers and provided solutions to a thousand logistic problems, in addition to offering many valuable suggestions in the orientation of the work.

In the months that followed I found myself many times in his little house behind the church in Hangaroa, partaking of a simple meal and discussing every aspect of the island's history. Many problems were thoroughly dissected and some were solved. I learned a great deal and I came to feel toward Father Sebastian much as the islanders did. Opportunities to continue these contacts occurred in 1960, when I returned with my family for a full year, and later during six-month visits in 1965-66 and 1968.

One of Father Sebastian's great dreams began to be realized in 1960 when work was started on the conservation and restoration of many of the monuments that had been so badly damaged in the internal warfare described in the final chapters of this book. For many years he had pointed out to anyone who would listen that Easter Island was potentially the most significant museum of art and architecture to be found anywhere in the Pacific. He hoped one day to see it conserved and maintained as a meaningful part of the world's cultural heritage and a commemoration of the prehistoric achievements of his beloved islanders. His industrous support to this end was given without reserve. He served as Honorary Chairman of the Easter Island Committee of the International Fund for Monuments, Inc., of New York, one of the organizations contributing to the conservation work. He made two trips to the United States and Canada, where he delivered public lectures and in many other ways aided in assembling funds. It was on his way home from the second of these trips that death overtook him in New Orleans on January 8, 1969.

In 1965 Father Sebastian mentioned to me that he had delivered a series of lectures by radio to the Arturo Prat Naval Base at Suberanía Bay on the Palmer Peninsula in Antarctica. It is a significant measure of the man that he, who had lived so many years in one of the most isolated of the world's communities, should feel concern for the loneliness of military personnel serving in Antarctica. When he was asked to help fill the leisure hours of these men by relating to them what he had learned about Easter Island, he agreed gladly. Special radio contact was established by the governor of the island, and the lectures were delivered irregularly, whenever conditions were favorable, between April and September of 1965. The contents of these lectures form the present book. I received Father Sebastian's permission to translate them from the Spanish and to prepare them for publication. Though he himself could perfectly well have translated them into English or any one of half a dozen languages, I had the advantage of easier access to contacts outside the island, and I have enjoyed the task thoroughly. This is the first of his important works to appear in English; others will surely follow.

The lectures made no pretense of new scientific contributions or of originality, though they contained significant information that is published nowhere else. Many of the topics had already been discussed by Father Sebastian in more precise and technical terms in *La Tierra de Hotu Matu'a* and other works. The lectures were exactly what they appear to be—an account of the history of Easter Island and its people directed to laymen, without technicalities of concern only to specialized scholars.

Father Sebastian delivered fourteen lectures, but in preparing them for publication in book form I have combined them into twelve chapters. Chapter 2 includes the second and third lectures, and Chapter 7 the eighth and ninth.

With a few of the statements in the following pages some professional students of the Pacific may disagree. I did not suggest to Father Sebastian that he modify or qualify any of these, for they represent the reasonable result of one independent line of investigation, and as such they have real value.

Among the disputable points is the time of arrival of Hotu Matu'a, the leader of the colonizing group with which the story begins. Father Sebastian's genealogical studies led him to the conclusion that Hotu Matu'a arrived some time in the sixteenth century, a reasonable view on the basis of his interpretation of the genealogies he used. Archaeological work has produced radiocarbon dates suggesting a longer occupation. The earliest of these is A.D. 857 plus or minus 200 years. This date appears to be associated with a large and complex religious structure that seems unlikely to have been among the earlier activities of colonists. Perhaps there were other people on the island before the arrival of Hotu Matu'a, or the genealogy may have lost many names. The events described in this book may have covered a greater time span than Father Sebastian suggests. On the other hand, the few early radiocarbon dates now available could be wildly in error. As yet the evidence is not conclusive.

There is much confusion about two groups of people, called respectively the Hanau Momoko and the Hanau Eepe, which figure in local traditions. Whether the Hanau Eepe arrived before, with, or after the Hanau Momoko is impossible to determine conclusively in the present state of knowledge and can be argued several ways. Father Sebastian's position that the Hanau Eepe were latecomers is at least as likely to be right as any other view. Whether the development of the gigantic outdoor altars called *ahu* was first stimulated by the Hanau Eepe, and the great statues were initially the work of the Hanau Momoko is also open to debate. Only in the future may the answers to these questions be found with certainty.

The political organization of the early Easter Island people may be somewhat confusing. The *ariki henua* was the most important person, but although he has sometimes been called a king, the individual holding that title appears not to have been a political leader but rather a repository of supernatural power and a religious symbol. The practical organization consisted of twelve local groups, eight of which appear to have been autonomous or nearly so. These were the Miru, Haumoana, Ngatimo, Marama, Ngaure, Ure o Hei, Tupahotu, and Koro Orongo. Three other groups, Raa, Hamea, and Hiti Uira, were subordinate to the Miru. Another, Mokomae, was subordinate to the Tupahotu. The Miru appear to have occupied a special position because they claimed direct descent from Hotu Matu'a, the first ariki henua. The local divisions were controlled by chiefs and people of special rank called *tangata honui;* the groups were further subdivided into an unknown number of what appear to have been patrilineal lineages.

As an organized adaptive pattern, the old way of life that Father Sebastian describes came to an end in the middle of the nineteenth century. The few survivors of disease and slave raids retained only shattered fragments of their former sophisticated culture. These have gradually disappeared under the influence of foreign contacts until only few and scattered memories remain today. The local language, though much contaminated by Spanish, Tahitian, and English words, is still spoken by one islander to another. As Spanish is taught in school, almost all the islanders know a good deal of it and many speak it perfectly. The more than 1400 people of today live by subsistence fishing and agriculture. Many have jobs in local administration, military detachments, and the developing tourism. A government-sponsored sheep ranch provides some public income.

The history of Easter Island is of unusual interest, because it shows what happened in one of the most isolated laboratories of human achievement to be found anywhere in the world. Here some of the most basic problems that beset mankind as a whole were confronted by a small group of vigorous and industrious people lacking the stimulation of outside ideas so typically fundamental to most human accomplishment elsewhere in the world. They arrived at many solutions and eventually reached a level of cultural complexity most unexpected in so isolated a community. In a typically human fashion their success appears to have carried with it the seeds of its own destruction. In the horrifying disintegration of the culture of this proud and successful people is reflected in microcosm the essence of the dilemma of twentieth-century man.

For the convenience of the reader some material has been added to supplement Father Sebastian's text. A Note on Pronunciation follows this foreword. The appendixes contain a list of the people mentioned; the genealogical list of ariki henua used by Father Sebastian; and a list of the places mentioned. Reference Notes, a Glossary, and a Selected Bibliography follow the appendixes.

The color photographs and some of the black and white photographs which illustrate the book were taken by George Holton, who first met Father Sebastian on Easter Island in 1967. Mr. Holton returned with his wife in 1968 on a trip made in cooperation with the International Fund for Monuments, Inc., which used many of his photographs in a fund-raising exhibit in New York City. The Holtons lived in a local house on Easter Island for several weeks and became good friends of Father Sebastian. Since he showed great interest in the photographs, it is singularly appropriate that a selection of them appears in this book.

A NOTE ON PRONUNCIATION

In the local language of Easter Island most letters are pronounced nearly as they are in Spanish, though the *r* is less trilled and sometimes suggests an *l* to English speakers. The *h* is sounded about as in English. The letters *ng*, which sometimes occur initially in words as well as elsewhere, are sounded about as they are in *song*. An apostrophe indicates a closure of the glottis. Double vowels indicate repeated sound values.

Vowels have approximately the following sound values:

> *a* as in *father*
> *e* as the "a" of *gray*
> *i* as the "e" of *me*
> *o* as in *go*
> *u* as in *rude*

Island at the Center of the World

~(ONE

Traditions, Records, and Geography

IN THIS BOOK I SHALL DISCUSS MANY TOPICS RELATING TO THE HISTORY OF Easter Island, this land of great statues and gigantic altars which has been of absorbing interest to me for more than thirty years. I hope my readers will be indulgent, for I can relate only what the people of the island have told me and what I have seen and read in the accounts of others. When the subject is enigmatic Easter Island no man's knowledge is either complete or secure.

To begin, I shall ask the reader to transport himself in spirit to this island in the month of April, 1936, during my second year of residence. It has been a year of unusual heat and long-continued drought, and there is little that is beautiful or attractive in the parched earth and dying banana plants which surround us. We are seated on a crude wooden bench in the scanty shade of the over-hanging roof of a dilapidated and malodorous leprosarium isolated some distance to the north of the village of Hangaroa where the rest of the island's inhabitants live. This old building has long been only a memory and today is replaced by a pleasant and commodious sani-tarium which houses and provides excellent medical attention for the few people who still suffer from leprosy. The lepers, who then numbered more than twenty, approach and sit around us. All are hideous with open sores, eroded noses, and mutilated hands and feet.

Some drag themselves to shady spots on their hands and knees. We are engaged in the oft-repeated ritual of listening to Arturo Teao, the oldest of the lepers, as he continues to relate his endless supply of traditions of the island's past, which I write down while brushing intermittently at the clouds of flies that settle on everything in sight including my hands and notebook.

Without doubt I have asked my reader to sit with me in an unpleasant place. To this day I remember it as an environment of gloom and hopelessness. Yet this memory is not entirely unmixed. I also remember fondly the good friends here who were able to relate to me traditions of the island's history which sparked a profound interest and which I was unable to hear anywhere else. These were people who remembered much and who gladly searched their memories to answer innumerable questions. I had tried in vain to find anyone in the village of Hangaroa who knew and could tell me in detail the traditions that by word of mouth had preserved through many generations the history of Easter Island. The people who lived in the village looked to the difficult problems of the present. They had no time for concern with the past, and it was little remembered. I gradually became aware that almost the only person who really cared very much about these stories out of the past for which I was searching was Arturo Teao, who had resided for more than twenty years in the leprosarium, having come there as a young man. His only companions were a few aged lepers. In this most isolated spot on the most isolated island in the Pacific these old people had no way to shorten the hours of their dull existence but to impart to this intelligent and alert youth their memories of what they had been told and what they had lived of the old times and the old way of life. As time passed Arturo became a living repository of the old traditions. He listened and he remembered, for he too had nothing else on which his active mind could dwell. One by one his teachers died and he became the only one to retain this knowledge. With what Arturo told me I began to develop my first glimmerings of insight into the fascinating and unlikely history of the island.

The head of a partially buried fallen moai at Rano Raraku

Totora reeds in the crater lake Rano Kau

Petroglyph of a fish; these are common on Easter Island

Naturally there were other sources of information. Other lepers and even people in the village were at length found to have some knowledge that could be pieced together to approach a coherent notion of past events. Much of this was fragmentary and contradictory. Stories learned from foreigners in recent times had been mingled with the authentic local legends, and the very human tendency to amplify and embellish a good story was often encountered. Even so, many accounts eventually could be checked against one another and some of the extraneous materials sifted out.

The first European explorers to visit the island left short but useful accounts, which, when compared with the island's artistic and architectural ruins and the stories of the islanders, became valuable documents. The first of these was the record in the ship's log kept by the Dutchman Jacob Roggeveen, who discovered the island on Easter Sunday of 1722 and named it in honor of the day. With Roggeveen came Carl Friedrich Behrens, who also wrote a narrative of the visit. In 1770 ships under the command of Felipe Gonzalez came to the island. In 1774, during his second voyage around the world, the English explorer Captain James Cook paid it a visit. He was followed in 1786 by the French Admiral Jean François de Galaup, Comte de La Pérouse. These three and others who accompanied them also reported their impressions. None had an opportunity to remain long, and their observations, as might be expected, were limited and thus are frustrating to the student of today. In some cases they did not understand what they saw and reported it imperfectly. Nevertheless these short records are of great value to us today as the only descriptions of the island culture as it was before being influenced by foreign contact. It is noteworthy that there is preserved among the local traditions a memory, dim though it may be, of each of these four visits. Without doubt they were even more memorable events to the islanders than to the explorers.

During the early and middle nineteenth century there were many more visitors, and we have more abundant written descriptions of the island and its people. Lamentably, some during this time came to exploit what they could find and behaved badly. As a natural result, the islanders developed considerable hostility toward outsiders. Other visitors met the hostility with dedication to the greater well-being of this remote community. The reports of greatest value during this period were written by the early missionaries, especially Brother Eugène Eyraud, who first brought Christianity to the island in 1864.

In the later nineteenth century the reports of systematic investigators began to be added to the observations of casual visitors. Their work has amplified in varying degrees what we can learn from other sources. The first important one was William J. Thomson, who, as paymaster of the American naval vessel *Mohican*, spent twelve days on the island at the end of 1886. With the aid of Alexander P. Salmon, a sheep rancher of mixed Tahitian and European ancestry, who in his long residence had learned much about the island and its people, Thomson recorded traditional information and also wrote detailed descriptions of some of the architectural monuments.

Between March 1914 and August 1915 an Englishwoman, Mrs. Scoresby Routledge, conducted an expedition which made observations on the contemporary people, collected additional traditional information, and provided extensive descriptions of the island's architectural monuments. Most of her notes were later lost, but her book *The Mystery of Easter Island* is a general popular work of real value.

In the latter half of 1934 a Franco-Belgian expedition brought Alfred Métraux and Henri Lavachery to Easter Island. Métraux produced a magnificent ethnological study of the island and its people. Lavachery carried out a number of archaeological investigations, his main contribution being a detailed record of the island's petroglyphs.

Between November 1955 and April 1956 a Norwegian expedition led by Thor Heyerdahl brought several professional archaeologists to the island. They completed a wide variety of systematic subsurface excavations and contributed greatly to our understanding of the prehistoric sequence of cultural development.

In the last six months of 1957 the German linguist Thomas Barthel recorded more traditional, cultural, and linguistic information. He spent many years both before and after this trip studying the enigmatic script with which the islanders wrote. The script and Barthel's book are discussed in Chapter 6.

In 1960 William Mulloy and Gonzalo Figueroa, who had accompanied the Heyerdahl expedition, returned on an expedition sent by the University of Chile. They spent the entire year surveying the architectural monuments with a view to determining means and methods for their conservation and restoration. As an experiment they completely restored two of the large outdoor altars, Ahu Vaiteka and Ahu Akivi, and re-erected the statues on these. Their work has an important bearing on the future of the island; the monuments need restoration badly, and, if properly preserved, they will one day become an archaeological museum without parallel in the Pacific.

Systematic archaeological research on Easter Island has barely begun. Even with the work that has already been accomplished, the great bulk of the monuments and other evidence of human activity remain uninvestigated. With modern archaeological techniques and radiocarbon and other methods of determining time much more of this remarkable story will be revealed in the future. But among the islanders all vestiges of the traditional knowledge of the past, so useful in explaining evidence recovered through archaeological excavation, will very soon have disappeared. The younger generation feels the effect of the twentieth century, and the past seems unimportant. For the islanders, increased contact with the new and exciting outside world is drawing a veil over the past as a winding sheet is drawn over a corpse.

Nevertheless, we already know something of the history of this remarkable mote of land in the vastness of the Pacific.

Easter Island's location is about 27 degrees south of the equator, and about 109 degrees west of Greenwich, and it is separated by great distances from any other inhabited land. It lies about 2,300 miles west of the continent of South America and about 1,400 miles east of Pitcairn Island, the nearest inhabited locality to the west. Thus the people who lived here were more isolated than those of many other Polynesian islands. The vast stretches of empty sea made contacts with other peoples rare indeed.

Located as it is near the northern border of the southern temperate zone, the island has a moderate climate with an average temperature of about 72 degrees Fahrenheit. Differences in temperature and rainfall between summer and winter are apparent though not sharp. In normal years a sufficient amount of rain (about 50 inches) falls in frequent local showers, so that the prehistoric inhabitants could cultivate the land without irrigation, as their descendants do today, and hope for sufficient harvests. As the island is without rivers or smaller streams, irrigation would have been impossible. But only in exceptionally dry years would there have been a scarcity of

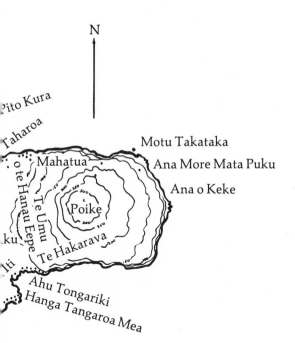

N

Pito Kura

Taharoa

Motu Takataka

Ana More Mata Puku

o te Hanau Eepe

Mahatua

Ana o Keke

Te Umu

Poike

ku

Te Hakarava

Iti

Ahu Tongariki

Hanga Tangaroa Mea

1 kilometer

contour interval 50 meters

· ahu

1.1″ = 1 mile

Easter Island (map by William Mulloy)

the fruits of the earth that, together with the products of the sea, constituted the principal food source.

The island rises from approximately the central part of a submarine volcanic elevation called the East Pacific Rise. On a spur of this same rise, about 210 miles to the east-northeast, is the tiny uninhabited islet of Sala y Gómez.

Easter Island is of volcanic origin and owes its triangular shape to three volcanoes that form its three corners. Rano Kau on the southwest, Maunga Terevaka on the northwest, and Poike on the east. Maunga Terevaka, the highest of these, has an elevation of about 1,700 feet. The slopes of these volcanoes form the island's interior, which consists of rolling country marked by many small satellite volcanic cones. There are many lava flows as well as extensive areas of excellent agricultural soil. The principal vegetation during historic times has been short grass with only a few small trees. In past times vegetation may have been much more luxuriant. Man himself, by cutting natural vegetation to make agricultural plots, may have been the principal agent in producing the present barren aspect.

There is no reef surrounding the island, and the coast is principally rocky cliffs, with few sandy beaches and no good anchorages.

Traditions, Records, and Geography   29

There are no flowing streams. The large freshwater lakes called Rano Kau, Rano Aroi, and Rano Raraku lie in volcanic craters and are covered with thick mats of *totora* reeds. The island is about 14 miles long by 7 miles wide and about 45 square miles in area.

In prehistoric times the inhabitants, who may have numbered 3,000 or 4,000, were organized in a kind of loose theocracy of very limited power which existed over all and left almost complete independence of action to the various kin-groups that resided in different sections of the island. There is no evidence that in prehistoric times the people were ever subjected to control from outside or had any need to fear foreign invaders. Distances were too great and contacts too infrequent to have made such dangers likely. Even in historic times, before 1888 there was only one attempt at foreign domination of the island. This resulted from the visit of the Spanish ships under Felipe Gonzalez in 1770. In a solemn ceremony these explorers took possession of the island in the name of Carlos III of Spain and named their acquisition San Carlos. They even secured the signatures of several of the local leaders among the islanders to their proclamation of possession.[1] The islanders certainly had no notion of what they were being asked to do, though they demonstrated their cultural advancement by writing their signatures in characters similar to those of the local *rongorongo* script which I shall discuss later. No Spanish colonization was ever carried out. These explorers, like other early visitors, were unable to see any means of economic exploitation of a colony so tiny and remote. Even the name San Carlos soon was lost. The island first acquired an outside political affiliation in 1888, when it became part of the Republic of Chile. Today Easter Island is part of the Province of Valparaíso.

In past times Easter Island has been known by several names. Its discovery on Easter Sunday of 1722 acounts for its most widely known one. In addition to San Carlos, Davis Island, Rapa Nui, Teapy, Whyhu, and others have also been used. The name I have always liked best is an early one used by the islanders themselves. They called their island Te Pito o Te Henua—The Navel [center] of the

World. One has only to climb to the summit of Maunga Terevaka, the northwest volcano and the island's highest point, and scan the sea horizon equidistant in every direction to understand why this is truly an island at the center of the world.

Racially the islanders are Polynesians. Easter Island forms the southwestern vertex of a huge triangle which has vertices also at Hawaii and New Zealand and is called the Polynesian Triangle; within this area lie all the islands on which Polynesian peoples live.

According to the history books, the Spanish explorer Álvaro de Mendaña de Neyra discovered the Marquesas about 1595; the English mariner Samuel Wallis discovered Tahiti in 1767; and Roggeveen, as I have mentioned, discovered Easter Island in 1722. This is obviously not strictly accurate. Many centuries before Balboa looked out over the Pacific from his summit in Darien or Magellan first traversed its waters, fearless navigators of another race had directed their canoes with unparalleled audacity over the immense reaches of this unknown sea to discover all the tiny islands within the Polynesian Triangle. When the belated Europeans first arrived they were met by thriving populations who had long been leading prosperous lives in these localities.

Who were the true discoverers of these beautiful islands? Whence did they come and in which direction did they sail? About the origin of these valiant seamen there are two principal theories, which are diametrically opposed and difficult to reconcile. One is that they were people of southeastern Asiatic origin, who sailed eastward, eventually to reach an ultimate frontier at Easter Island. The other is that they were American Indians who sailed westward to use Easter Island, Hawaii, and the Marquesas as staging areas for further penetrations among the islands of Polynesia. The conflicting theories, passionately and violently debated by the students of the Pacific, are discussed in Chapter 2.

TWO

Where Did the Polynesians Originate?

WHETHER THE SETTLERS OF THE POLYNESIAN ISLANDS SAILED WESTWARD FROM America or eastward from Asia is a question which cannot be given a conclusive answer on the evidence now at hand. A good deal is known about peoples who in recent times have lived on many of the Pacific islands. Their archaeological history, on the other hand, is only beginning to be studied. It is from this latter kind of information that convincing evidence of prehistoric movements will be derived. Perhaps there is truth in both theories, and only by combining them can students reach a full understanding of this saga of human ingenuity and fortitude against the natural forces of the greatest of all oceans.

Most students hold the view that the ancestors of the Polynesians were Asiatics who once lived in Indonesia and earlier on the Asian continent. Long ago in this coastal and island environment they became skilled fishermen and seafarers and eventually developed skills and equipment to make the long voyages necessary to discover islands progressively farther east and farther apart.

Perhaps the most widely known exponent of this view was the late Sir Peter Buck (Te Rangi Hiroa) who made the most famous exposition of it in his book *Vikings of the Sunrise*. He was a remarkable personality well fitted for the investigations he carried out. Born in New Zealand in 1880 of a Maori mother and an Irish father, he obtained a medical degree from New Zealand University and served with distinction as Medical Health Officer with the Maori and later in the New Zealand Parliament. An absorbing interest in the history of the peoples of the Pacific finally caused him to give up his medical pursuits and become associated with the Bernice P. Bishop Museum in Honolulu where he held the post of director at the time of his death in 1951. His work was strongly colored by his Maori heritage, and this provided him with knowledge and insights of tremendous value. He always used his Maori name as well as his English one on his published works.

Essentially his views about the origin of the Polynesians were these: Southeastern Asia and the adjacent islands of Indonesia have had a complicated racial and cultural history. Among early residents were Pygmy Negritos who were once widely distributed; remnants of these survive today in a few of the isolated localities such as northern Luzon, the Malay Peninsula, and the interior of New Guinea. Later, Oceanic Negroes lived widely in the region and are found today in the islands of Melanesia around the northern and eastern shores of Australia. Still later the area was occupied by brown-skinned, wavy-haired, Caucasian people remotely related to the Caucasians in Europe, North Africa, and southwestern Asia. Buck believed that these people came to Indonesia from India. Later students have favored southern China and adjacent localities. Whatever their origin, they developed numerous agricultural and fishing communities in Indonesia. They appear to have spoken Malayo-Polynesian languages related to languages spoken today everywhere in Polynesia.

Their economy was based on root and fruit crops, such as yams, breadfruit, sugar cane, taro, coconut, banana, and the paper mulberry from which they made bark cloth. Fishing was highly important. Domestic animals included pigs, chickens, and dogs. Cooking was done by boiling in bamboo tubes and baking with hot stones in earth ovens. Most things they used were made of perishable materials— wood, bamboo, and fibers. Wood carving and other wood working were highly developed. The most common stone implements were chisels and adzes. Weapons included a variety of clubs and spears. Stones were thrown with slings. Houses probably varied but basically were simple rectangular thatched-roofed structures with pole frames, sometimes elevated on posts and sometimes built on stone platforms.

They were probably organized in village kin-groups with a simple political structure, and with chiefs who did not exercise much power. Judging by later Indonesian survivals, they would have had deep respect for ancestors and the belief that these were important to the welfare of the living. The concept of taboo (on Easter Island *tapu*) was strongly developed. With these were widespread beliefs in deities controlling various forces of nature.

As time passed, Mongoloid peoples began to move in from the continent and gradually to change the racial character of the population. At the same time communities to which fishing was important were undergoing vital training in seafaring in the course of their local interisland fishing trips. Small dugout canoes were gradually developed into true seagoing sailing vessels. Planks, carefully adzed to a precise fit and sewn into place with fibers, were added to the sides of vessels to provide greater freeboard. The boat builders learned to use the stabilizing device known as the outrigger, which consisted of a log float resting on the water parallel to the canoe and attached to it by two light poles. Eventually the stabilizing effect of the outrigger suggested its replacement by a second canoe, and, with the intervening space decked over, the seaworthy double canoe was born. Effective sails were developed and the size of the vessels was increased until they became capable of making long voyages. Experience produced extensive knowledge of stars, winds, and the total environment of the sea which made possible navigation out of sight of land. Finally, the time came to push outward in the greatest nautical adventure in all human history. Some seamen traveled northward as far as Japan. Others sailed westward to reach Madagascar and East Africa. Still others turned their faces eastward toward the Pacific. Transport canoes used in Polynesian colonization are said to have measured up

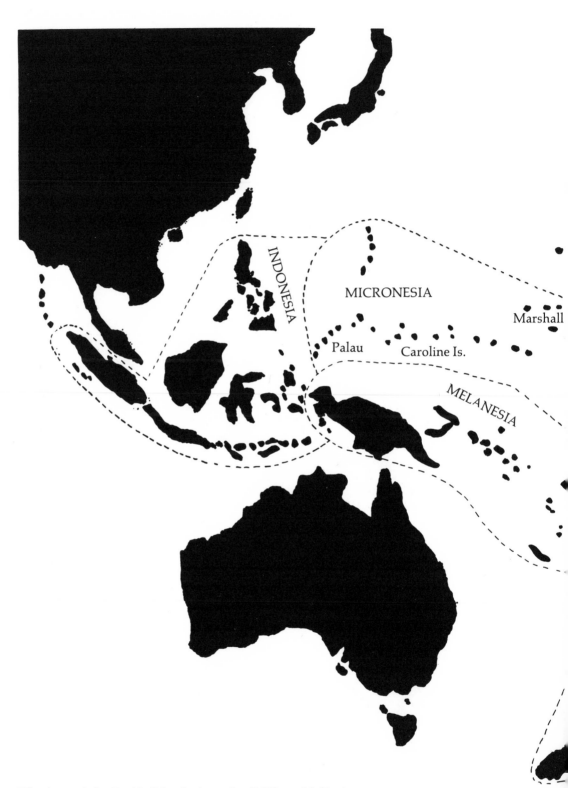

The area of the Pacific Islands (map by William Mulloy)

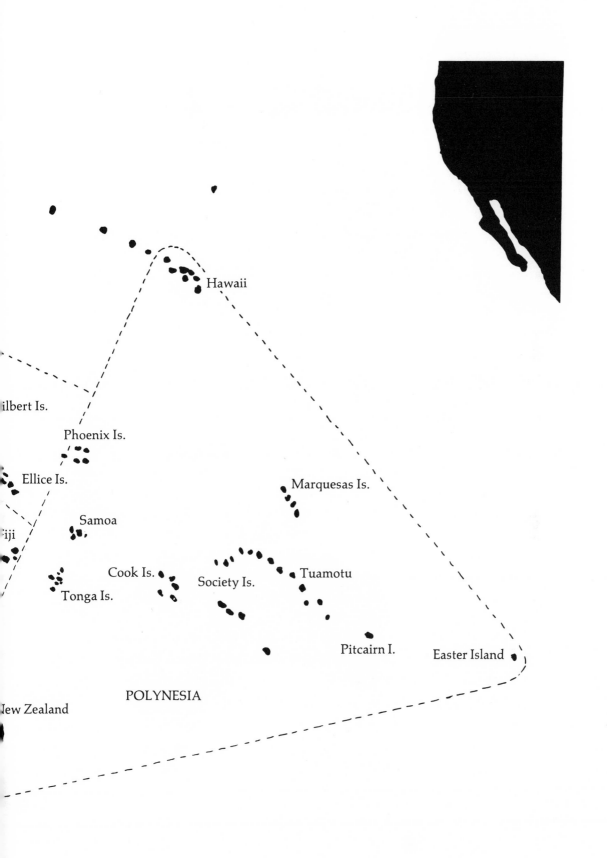

Hawaii

ilbert Is.

Phoenix Is.

Ellice Is.

Marquesas Is.

Samoa

iji

Cook Is.

Society Is.

Tuamotu

Tonga Is.

Pitcairn I.

Easter Island

POLYNESIA

lew Zealand

to 80 feet. Being double canoes connected by decks, these could accommodate sixty or more people, with their provisions, plants, pigs, dogs, and chickens. According to traditions which I shall discuss later, such a double canoe carried the first immigrants with their leader, the *ariki henua* Hotu Matu'a, to Easter Island.

It was Buck's view that this eastward movement out of Indonesia passed first through the tiny islands of Micronesia: Yap, Palau, and the Carolines which lie north and west of most of Polynesia. Some explorers continued to the northeast, eventually to reach Hawaii. Others passed southward through the Gilbert and Phoenix islands and eventually reached central Polynesia. Buck believed the vanguard reached this point around the fifth century A.D.; radiocarbon dates now indicate an earlier arrival. According to Buck, colonists established themselves on the island of Raiatea (formerly called Havaiki), in the Society group, which was for a time the cultural focus of central Polynesia. They planted cuttings carefully brought with them and established flourishing communities. From there navigators spread out in all directions to explore unknown seas and discover new islands. Tahiti to the east, also in the Society group, soon became known, and later New Zealand, the Cook and Tonga islands, the Tuamotus, and the Marquesas. Though Buck's view strongly favors entry into Polynesia by way of Micronesia, other students believe that there were several movements, of which one, perhaps the earliest, passed north of New Guinea to enter Polynesia by way of Fiji, Tonga, and Samoa. This latter route passes among high volcanic islands, which would explain how many imported crops, difficult or impossible to cultivate on the low coral atolls of Micronesia, could have survived the trip to Polynesia.

Of especial interest is Buck's view of the source of the Easter Island population. Taking account of a tradition, which I shall relate later, of two distinctive groups, one called the "long ears" and the other the "short ears" (both terms erroneous), Buck believed that the former came from the Marquesas where the custom of enlarging the lobes of the ears was practiced and the latter from the Gambier group of the Tuamotus to the west, of which the principal island is Mangareva.

Buck also suggested that eastward Polynesian penetration did not end at Easter Island. Two of the historically most interesting plants cultivated in Polynesia are the sweet potato (*Ipomoea batatas*), which in Chile is called *camote*, and the bottle gourd (*Lagenaria siceraria*), both of which appear to be of South American origin. In the case of the sweet potato the name *kumara* used on Easter Island and elsewhere in Polynesia is similar to that used in Peru. Buck suggests that these plants may have been brought to Polynesia as the result of a single voyage to the Peruvian coast, most likely made by Marquesans. A single uninterrupted voyage of almost 4,000 miles and return is difficult to imagine, but it might have happened.

For the general idea of the peopling of the Pacific by migrants from Indonesia there is much evidence, and most students hold some variation of this. Malayo-Polynesian languages spoken universally in Polynesia clearly are derived from Indonesia. This is impressive evidence and cannot be explained on any basis other than contact. The bulk of Polynesian food and other utilized plants appear to have originated there. Most tools, weapons, utensils, and other manufactured items, as well as social, political, and religious ideas of Polynesia, have counterparts in Indonesia. Such thorough-going cultural similarities make it difficult to doubt that some sort of intense contact took place.

This, however, may not tell the whole story. A number of cultural elements in Polynesia in addition to the cultivation of the bottle gourd and sweet potato suggest contacts with South America. This brings us to the question of the penetration of American Indians into the Pacific.

The chief proponent of the theory that such penetration occurred is Thor Heyerdahl, who, like Buck, is a truly remarkable man. Born in Larvik, Norway, in 1914, he seems to carry in his veins some of the blood of Leif Ericson. Heyerdahl is, however, much more than an adventurer and explorer of far-off lands; he is also a serious and well-informed investigator of the history of the Pacific. Shortly after finishing his studies in zoology at the University of Oslo he fled from civilization with his wife to live on an isolated island. By way of Tahiti the couple arrived in 1936 at Fatu Hiva in the Marquesas. Here they lived for more than a year in close relationship with nature and the local people. This stay in Fatu Hiva had decisive influence on Heyerdahl's future. There he was told by an old man called Tei Tetua a legend of how the first inhabitants of those islands had come from a country to the east, on the other side of the sea, under the command of a divine king called Tiki. The magic of this legend set Heyerdahl's subsequent course through an unusually active lifetime of study and investigation. He devoted most of the next decade to study of American Indian and Pacific literature in search of evidence of New World-Pacific contacts.

Among Peruvian legends dating from a period long before the Inca empire he found an account of a certain Kon Tiki, a name which signified "Tiki of the Sun," who ruled a domain in the vicinity of Lake Titicaca. Kon Tiki was defeated in battle and fled with some loyal companions to the Peruvian coast. There he built a raft and sailed west. Heyerdahl became strongly impressed with the idea that the Peruvian Kon Tiki might be the same as the Tiki of the Marquesan legend. Setting out to investigate this possibility, he found evidence that peoples of the central Andean coastal region in prehistoric times had built sailing rafts that were capable of extended sea voyages. Even so, a trip to Polynesia seemed an incredible journey. Heyerdahl resolved to see if it could be done.

At the end of the second World War he came with four companions to Ecuador to build a raft designed according to what he knew of the prehistoric vessels. He and his companions cut huge balsa logs in the interior and floated them to the coast. There they constructed the raft, with a large square sail and peculiar Peruvian centerboards made of vertical planks passed downward between the logs.

He named the vessel *Kon-Tiki*, and on April 28, 1947, he and his companions sailed westward from Callao. They had the advantage of the prevailing southeasterly winds and the westward drift of the Humboldt current, which would have been of similar service to prehistoric Indians in making the same voyage. After 101 days they arrived at Raroia in the Tuamotu Archipelago. Being unable to maneuver to reach an opening in the reef, they had to pass over the sharp coral. The raft was wrecked, and the occupants were thrown into the lagoon, whence they easily reached shore. Actually the raft probably would have landed safely had Heyerdahl then known how to operate the curious Peruvian centerboards. He found later that by raising or lowering one or another of these vertical planks the raft could be sailed surprisingly close to the wind. Apparently it was a more seaworthy vessel than even he knew at the time of his trip.

This was a clear demonstration that Indians could have sailed to Polynesia. However, Heyerdahl carefully pointed out in his book *Kon-Tiki* that the trip did not constitute proof that such migrations ever took place, but only that they were possible with equipment known to American Indians.[1]

Comparative studies of American Indian and Pacific cultures led Heyerdahl further to believe that South Americans were later followed by other Indians from the North American coast, who came first to Hawaii and later to other islands farther south.

In 1952 Heyerdahl published a voluminous work entitled *American Indians in the Pacific*, in which his views were expressed in detail. He attempted to support them with detailed comparative studies of legends, religious ideas, stone sculpture, boatbuilding, physical characteristics, and cultivated plants. Much of his reasoning was considered overdrawn by other students, and he was accused of ignoring evidence not in accord with his theory.

Publication of *Kon-Tiki* had brought Heyerdahl not only fame but considerable financial return. This latter he used freely to continue his investigations. In 1953, accompanied by two archaeologists, he carried out excavations in the Galápagos Islands off the coast of

Ecuador. *Archaeological Evidence of Pre-Spanish Visits to the Galá-pagos Islands*, written in collaboration with Arne Skjölsvold, demonstrates that prehistoric Indians reached at least this island group a little more than 600 miles from the South American coast.

In 1955 and 1956 Heyerdahl led a more important expedition to Easter Island and other islands of the eastern Pacific, on which he was accompanied by five archaeologists. The group worked on Easter Island for a little over five months. Detailed excavations were made of religious structures, villages, caves, the great statue quarry at Rano Raraku, and various other sites. The expedition later visited Pitcairn Island, Mangareva, Rapa Iti, Tubuai, Raivavae, the Marquesas, and other islands.

Heyerdahl's next publication, *Aku-Aku*, was another best-seller. This was translated into many languages, but it is of little scientific value. Because descriptions of actual facts are somewhat mixed with exaggerations and above all with a few not entirely reliable accounts collected from certain islanders, it placed the author in some danger of losing his reputation as a serious investigator. Nevertheless, the book is well written and makes fascinating reading for those who like mystery stories.

Happily Heyerdahl's reputation has been fully vindicated by the truly important work *Archaeology of Easter Island*, which he edited in collaboration with Edwin Ferdon. This is a collection of monographs dealing with various aspects of the island's archaeology, written by Heyerdahl and the archaeologists who accompanied him on the expedition I mentioned earlier. It includes detailed descriptions of the excavation of several *ahu* or large outdoor altars bearing gigantic statues. The statue quarry at Rano Raraku was investigated, and much was learned about the carving of the gigantic statues. The ceremonial village of Orongo was investigated. Excavations were carried out at the Poike ditch (Te Umu o te Hanau Eepe), the traditional site of a great battle between two groups of islanders. (I shall discuss all these later.) The results of the work of Heyerdahl and his party are undoubtedly of great importance to an understanding of Easter Island's prehistory.

Heyerdahl's views in the terms in which he has presented them have found few supporters among anthropologists. Yet he has contributed a great service by the investigations he has made possible and in calling attention to the possibility of New World influences at least on eastern Polynesia. Even Buck could not ignore such American plants as the bottle gourd and the sweet potato which must have been introduced by man. Other plants are equally suggestive, though evidence for their origin is not so clear. Among these are the *totora* reed, which grows in the crater lakes of Easter Island, and Hawaiian cotton. Though Heyerdahl has been accused of going beyond the reasonable in parallels he has drawn, some are at least enough to cause the thoughtful investigator to maintain an open mind as to possibilities of influences from the New World. The precisely fitted stone work of the famous ahu at Vinapu on Easter Island, which I describe later, is highly reminiscent of some of the masonry found in Peru. The idea of gigantic stone statues appears centered in eastern Polynesia and has parallels in western South America, though there are few detailed similarities of style. Probably the reason that most students find it difficult to accept the notion of New World contacts with Polynesia is that there are relatively few direct parallels with New World cultures. No American Indian languages have been found in the Pacific, nor have New World pottery, emphasis on woven clothing, continental types of stone tools, metal objects, most New World cultivated plants, and similar items that might be expected.

When future archaeological work has provided new evidence, it may appear that Easter Island and other islands in eastern Polynesia represent a kind of meeting place of influences from both east and west. Perhaps the seemingly unreconcilable views of Buck and Heyerdahl may both contain elements of truth. One day they may complement each other to reveal fuller understanding of the mysterious Polynesians.

THREE

Man Comes to Easter Island

AN OLD TRADITION, RELATED TO ME MANY TIMES, DESCRIBES THE BIRTH IN ITS present form of the island anciently called Te Pito o Te Henua. According to the story, a potent supernatural being named Uoke, who came from a place called Hiva, for reasons unknown traveled about the Pacific with a gigantic lever with which he pried up whole islands and tossed them into the sea where they vanished forever under the waves. After thus destroying many islands he came at length to the coast of Te Pito o Te Henua, then a much larger land than it is today. He began to lever up parts of it and cast them into the sea. Eventually he reached a place called Puko Puhipuhi, which is still pointed out by the local people in the vicinity of Hanga Hoonu. Here the rocks of the island were too sturdy for Uoke's lever, and it was broken against them. He was unable to dispose of the last fragment, and this remained as the island we know today. Thus Te Pito o Te Henua continues to exist only through the accident of Uoke's broken lever.

Though the story of Uoke and his lever, like many legends, appears fanciful to people of today, it may contain a grain of historical truth. Like the Greek gods Hephaestus, god of fire, who resided in the depths of the volcano called Etna, and Poseidon, god of the sea, who produced its violent movements with his enormous trident, Uoke appears to be a kind of personification of such destructive forces of nature as the catastrophes that produce volcanic eruptions and tidal waves. As the Pacific islands are products of vulcanism, those who dwell on them are accustomed to such manifestations.

It is not necessary to evoke stories of now sunken continents to understand the stimulus that produced the story of Uoke. Islands have sunk and reappeared again even in modern times, and volcanic eruptions in the Pacific are not soon forgotten by any who see them. Recent geological studies have admitted the possibility that there may have been volcanic eruptions on Easter Island within the period of human occupation, and indeed the future may still bring others. In 1960 a gigantic tidal wave, developed by the devastating earthquakes in continental Chile, struck the island in a wall of water many feet high with such force as to carry 60-ton stone statues a hundred yards inland and dash them to the ground. The work of Uoke's lever is thus still to be seen occasionally on this island as well as on others.

The word Hiva, mentioned in the legend as the name of the place from which Uoke came, is also the name of the traditional earlier homeland of at least some of the people of this island. The same word has also been preserved in the names of three of the Marquesas Islands—Nuku Hiva, Fatu Hiva, and Hiva Oa. Perhaps that area was the Hiva of the Easter Islanders. Considerable archaeological evidence suggests that this is at least a likely possibility. It is also noteworthy that the memory of the existence of a place called Hiva is found in the old name of the islet of Sala y Gómez, which I mentioned earlier as lying some 210 miles east-northeast of Easter Island. The earlier islanders knew this tiny rock by the name of Motu Motiro Hiva. The most probable translation of this phrase is "islet located in front of Hiva." Heyerdahl has pointed out that this old name suggests that Hiva lay somewhere to the east and could thus be only the South American continent. Today the islanders do not know where Hiva lies; they remember it only as the place from which their ancestors came. In modern times all foreigners, regardless of their origin, are called *tangata hiva,* which means "men from Hiva."

Two versions of the tradition related to me give different reasons why the great Polynesian king, or ariki henua, Hotu Matu'a, set sail for the navel of the world. One tells of a great cataclysm in Hiva, in which most of the land, also through the mischief of Uoke's lever, was submerged under the sea. Here again only a remnant, called Maori, which was the part of Hiva in which Hotu Matu'a lived, was left. The locality in Maori in which his home lay was called Marae Renga. The other version states that the principal reason for the departure of Hotu Matu'a was family trouble, chiefly instigated by his brother Oroi. This legend relates that a certain Hau Maka in Hiva saw in a dream the future land of Hotu Matu'a. In the spirit, Hau Maka traveled over the whole of the island, observing everything and searching out the best beach for the future landing. He traveled westward along the north coast and studied the beaches at Taharoa, Hanga Hoonu, and Ovahe. Finally he saw the pink sand at Anakena and said, "Here is the great beach where Hotu Matu'a will touch the shore." His spirit returned to Hiva, and upon awakening he said to a youth called Ira, "There is an island in the direction of the sun. Go and look at the island where Hotu Matu'a will live."

The name of Hau Maka is one of the few old ones still remembered vividly by the islanders of today. His memory is kept alive in a song which recounts part of the legend:

O Hotu Matu'a i-unga-mai ai	Hotu Matu'a sent here
Ia Hau Maka, i toona tuura	His servant Hau Maka
Ka-kimi te maara mo te ariki	To search out a landing place
Mo te ariki, mo tomo.	For the king to land.

As other Polynesian voyagers frequently appear to have done, Hau Maka, traditionally, sent out a reconnaissance voyage from Hiva. Seven youths, including Ira who had first been told to go, were sent to explore the land that Hau Maka had seen in his dream. They are said to have sailed toward the sun. This ambiguous statement could be interpreted to mean that they sailed either east or west, but information in the legend which I shall mention later leaves no doubt that their voyage was toward the rising sun.

That seven young men were sent venturing over an extensive unknown sea in search of land only vaguely described and that they were able to carry out their mission is no more than typical of this intrepid race of navigators. Some details of the tradition make them appear to be irresponsible rogues. After arriving at Easter Island they treated heartlessly and without compassion one of their number named Ku'uku'u who was wounded by the flippers of a supernatural turtle that had come from Hiva. He was carried to a low cave and callously abandoned to his fate. A small cave near Anakena is still pointed out as the place where he spent his last hours. It is related that Ku'uku'u planted yams on the slopes of Rano Kau at a place that is still known as Ko te Uhi a Ku'uku'u, or "the yam plantation of Ku'uku'u." When they saw that the yams that were to feed the future colonists had been invaded by weeds, the members of the group decided to abandon its mission and return to Hiva.

Five of them were making ready to leave the island, which they had come to consider uninviting and poorly endowed, when, on awakening one morning, they saw near the islet of Motu Nui the double canoe of Hotu Matu'a. When it was a short distance from the coast, the vessel was hailed by Ira, who recommended that a reconnaissance around the coast be made. The voyagers cut the lashings that held the two canoes together and allowed them to continue their courses separately. This might have been done to facilitate landing on the mostly rockbound island coast. In one canoe, called *Oteka*, came Hotu Matu'a with his wife Vakai a Heva. In the other, called *Oua*, came his sister Ava Rei Pua with her husband, who, according to one perhaps not very reliable version of the legend, was the famous nobleman, or *ariki*, called Tu'u ko Iho, who was later remembered as the first carver of the unique wooden statues called *moai kavakava*. I shall discuss these statues later. In each of the canoes came also many colonists.

Hotu Matu'a in the canoe *Oteka* continued eastward along the southern coast of the island and returned along the north coast to disembark at Anakena beach near the center of the north coast. The canoe *Oua* turned north along the west coast and thence east along the north coast to follow the shorter route to Anakena. Noting that *Oua* was about to arrive first, Hotu Matu'a called upon his *mana*, the magical power possessed by the members of the royal lineage and by the ariki or nobles. He pronounced a spell that slowed the progress of *Oua* until his own canoe touched the beach.

At the beautiful horseshoe-shaped bay at Anakena, Hotu Matu'a anchored *Oteka* on the east side close to the point still called Hiro Moko. *Oua* was moored at the other side of the bay at a place called Hanga o Hiro.

On the day of the arrival two infants were born. In the canoe *Oteka*, Vakai a Heva gave birth to a son to whom Hotu Matu'a gave the name Tu'u Maheke. In *Oua* a daughter was born to Ava Rei Pua. The legend relates the events of the birth of Tu'u Maheke in great detail. As the canoe passed Taharoa the vaginal mucus appeared, as it passed Hanga Hoonu the mucus plug was delivered, and upon arrival at Anakena the amniotic fluid flowed out. It is unfortunate that many other aspects of the events of the arrival were not remembered in similar detail.

Close to the beach where Hotu Matu'a and his people disembarked is still to be seen the cave called Anakena (*ana kena*)—"the cave of *kena* bird." Here Hotu Matu'a remained with his family until his retainers could build a house for him. The name of this cave now designates the entire beach and the surrounding area. In earlier times the bay was called Hanga Kaupari a Morie Roa.

With Hotu Matu'a came a master builder of the distinctive Easter Island houses (*hare paenga*) which I shall describe later. His name was Nuku Kehu. Of him the tradition speaks thus: "The wife of Nuku Kehu remained in Hiva. She was called Maramara Kai. Nuku Kehu remembered her fondly and was always unhappy when the sun set in the direction of Hiva where Maramara Kai lived." This small memory of the personal sadness of a husband longing for his wife is historically most interesting, because it leaves no doubt that the immigrants traveled in the direction of the rising sun.

Eventually Nuku Kehu built a house at Anakena for Hotu Matu'a. It was called Tupo Tu'u. Another was built nearby for his wife. Hotu Matu'a intended that this beautiful beach should be his home and that of his successors—here they would live with their tu'ura, or retainers, who ceremonially took care of all their needs. Some unusually well-shaped and precisely fitted stones of the foundation of a large house, which the islanders say was that of Hotu Matu'a, can be seen today. The house is largely destroyed, and many of the beautifully cut stones have been carried away, but originally it must have been about 160 feet long.

The place in which the ariki henua lived with his family was tapu, or sacred, as were their own persons. Tapu, or taboo, is generally a kind of negative magic or prohibition which frequently refers to a person who must not be touched, a thing which must not be used, or a place in which it is not permitted to set foot. This concept was an important element in the religious practice on most islands of Polynesia and was vitally important on Easter Island. The mana with which Hotu Matu'a delayed the canoe called *Oua* was a kind of impersonal supernatural power possessed by the ariki. With it they enforced tapu, and it was an important source of their prestige among their people. Mana was thought to be a power that not only enforced prohibitions but also resulted in many kinds of advantages to the communities at large. Because of mana the crops grew well, the chickens multiplied rapidly, fish were abundant in the sea, and turtles came to the beach. The heads of the ariki were thought to be especially endowed with such mana, and this remained potent after their deaths. It was customary to identify the skulls of the ariki by incising certain signs on their foreheads. These skulls were sometimes stolen and hidden in plantations or chicken houses to increase production. This is a significant key to understanding the true nature of mana. It existed completely outside the volition of the possessor, who was essentially its receptacle or vehicle. Though presumably the ariki would not have wanted their skulls to be stolen from their graves, the power inherent in these nevertheless served perfectly well the ends of the successful thief.

The notions of tapu and mana are still understood by many islanders, but they consider these to have been deprived of their potency by the introduction of Christianity. During the time of the early missionaries there remained on the island a member of the royal family—a young boy called Rokoroko he Tau. Like those of all the ariki, his head was considered to be tapu, and therefore it was not permitted to cut his hair. When the missionary Father Hyppolyte Roussel, who cared for the boy in his last illness, wanted to cut his hair for hygienic reasons, he encountered tenacious resistance. He was threatened with having stones thrown at him by a community violent in its defense of the ancient privilege of its ruler's head to be untouchable.[1]

Hotu Matu'a and later ariki henua thus lived in sacred isolation and exercised little or no political power. Their function was not that of kings as we usually think of them. They were respected as people of superior rank and as repositories of mana that could be expected to provide important benefits for everyone.

Most of the people who came with Hotu Matu'a appear to have moved immediately to other localities where they began to establish new communities. Eventually they came to form eight distinctive kin-groups, each with its own name. Each had its own persons of rank, called *tangata honui*. Under these, in later times at least, were several classes of people, including war leaders, priests, craftsmen, farmers, and fishermen. Their system was clearly that of a class-organized or stratified society.

As soon as the new colonists had landed on Anakena beach, quite naturally their first concern was to develop a secure food supply. Planting, building, and the many tasks that are the lot of the pioneer were waiting to be done.

✦ FOUR

Building a New Life

IN ALL THE PREHISTORIC COLONIZING VOYAGES OF THE POLYNESIANS NOTHING was more important than attention to the living plants that were carried along to be planted in the new land. The natural vegetation of Pacific islands has little to offer that is edible, and the ability to maintain living plants at sea and to establish them in new soil meant quite simply the difference between survival and death.

Typically, the tradition states that not only did the reconnaissance party devote its first attention to the planting of yams, but the people of Hotu Matu'a had hardly set foot on shore before they too began to plant. The legend does not mention that they found many surviving edible plants, and it would seem that the yams planted by the advance party did not grow or were insufficient, for the account relates that for the first three months the colonists had nothing to eat but fish and sandalwood nuts called *moki oone*. These latter, which today are extinct on the island, were probably transmitted to this remote spot by natural means in much earlier times. The tree called *makoi nau opata* that produced them was still occasionally found in a few localities as late as 1895, but its last representatives are now dead. Today only shells of the nuts are occasionally found in dry caves. Behrens was probably referring to the fruit of the sandalwood when he said that the islanders gave many nuts to Roggeveen's crew.[1]

At the time that the people of Hotu Matu'a began their cultivation, the natural vegetation may have been very different from that which lends the island its barren and windswept aspect today. The first task may have been to grub out a heavy bush. Recent pollen studies have suggested that there may once have been a thick forest, including palms and conifers and many other species now locally extinct.[2] This would have to have been cleared to make plantations, and as ever more land was needed to support an increasing population the more luxuriant vegetation may well have been destroyed until none was left. When the land ceased to be cultivated, the short grass of today would be a natural replacement for the crops.

The task of cultivation was not easy. The climate was presumably less tropical than in Hiva, and the rich soil was as if sowed with stones of volcanic lava. The saying of the early rabbis that when God created the earth he had two sacks of stones in his hands, of which he dumped one over Palestine and the other over the rest of the world cannot be wholly correct. Surely God emptied at least one well-filled sack over Easter Island.

The islanders did not know cereals or bread. In place of these they used yams, taro, and sweet potatoes. When the early missionaries translated the Lord's Prayer into the local language they had to substitute "our daily food" for "our daily bread." Though yams are little cultivated today, in earlier times over forty varieties were known. There were fourteen varieties of taro and twenty-five varieties of sweet potatoes. All these may not have been true botanical variants, but they were distinguished by name.

It would seem that in earlier times the yam was most cultivated, for in the version of the tradition related by Arturo Teao, which is the most complete one, only this tuber is mentioned by name as having been brought by the people of Hotu Matu'a. Undoubtedly other plants were brought also, but apparently only this one merited mention.

A tradition told to me relates the typically Polynesian astuteness of a certain Teke, who was charged with providing the party with samples of all the available kinds of yams before it set out from Hiva. During the last night on shore, before they loaded the canoes, he asked his companions to dig up the yams that had just been planted by a man called Maeha. While the field was being despoiled, Teke kept Maeha engaged in conversation throughout the night. In the morning they went out to look at the ravaged field, and while Teke disclaimed knowledge of the depredation, Maeha sadly began to take in his hands one by one the remains of the broken yams that had been discarded. Holding the first of these he exclaimed, "I have in my hand the yam *hatuke* that belonged to Maeha." Teke thought to himself, "The yam hatuke that was Maeha's now belongs to Teke." As Maeha pronounced the name of each yam Teke learned the names of all those that had been taken. These names were preserved on Easter Island.

Climate did not permit the cultivation of the breadfruit so valuable in other parts of Polynesia. The coconut, here called niu, did not do well either, and only a few trees grew. The banana grew successfully. Many plantations were made, and it became an important source of food. Today the islanders still grow the five varieties brought by their ancestors, which are clearly distinguishable by their form and taste from those which have been more recently introduced.

To make life sweet the colonists planted sugar cane and *ti*. This latter large-leafed plant provides a root that when cooked is as sweet as molasses and is a welcome supplement to any meal. Taro, a large, slender, white tuber much like a potato in taste, was also known from early times, although the people here do not appear to have mashed it to make *poi poi* as people do on many other Polynesian islands. All three of these plants are still used. The products of the soil are known on Easter Island as *inaki*, or that which serves to accompany the principal food, which today is fish or meat.

The prehistoric islanders had little mammalian meat. The *kio'e*, or Polynesian rat, was present. There is no legendary record of its having been brought by the colonists, though it must have been transported by man. The chicken appears to have been brought by the colonists, but there is no mention of pigs or dogs, other Polynesian animals that might have been expected. These latter appear not to have been known on the island in prehistoric times. In 1786, La Pérouse tried to remedy the problem of meat by leaving a gift of goats and sheep on the island.[3] These were evidently immediately eaten or left no issue. The people did not understand the intent of the good admiral. There remains only a possible memento of this kind deed in paintings, now unhappily mostly destroyed, on the walls of the cave called Ana Kai Tangata. A three-masted European ship is pictured and near it the figure of a sheep.

The tradition describes Hotu Matu'a as longing for his native Hiva and remembering it as "a land of much food and greasy lips," where they ate the flesh of the *kekepu*. We do not know what animal the kekepu was; it may well have been the pig.

Because of lack of other meat the chicken was much more important here than on many Polynesian islands. Chickens must have been raised in great numbers. Prominent among the gifts offered to the early European visitors were many chickens. Roggeveen said that the islanders brought a great abundance of sugar cane, chickens, yams, and bananas.[4] Behrens, who was with him, added that they brought "us a quantity of dressed fowls"; and later that "they brought us more than 500 live fowls."[5]

The island is poor today in comparison with its earlier poultry production. Everywhere one sees near the prehistoric domestic establishments the abandoned chicken houses, or *hare moa*, of long ago. These are massive, flat-topped, rectangular structures of heavy stone masonry, typically about 26 by 7 feet in extent and 7 feet high. They have a small chamber inside and a lateral entrance large enough to admit a chicken. Chickens were placed inside each night. The chicken houses were so built to foil thieves who found that getting at the fowls involved a prohibitive amount of noisy dismantling of masonry.

Fishing was important, though more difficult on Easter Island than in many parts of the Pacific, since the island has no encircling coral reef and thus no lagoon. Fishing had to be done in the open sea or along the shore. The large tuna, called *kahi,* and similar fish that are encountered in the *haka no nonga,* or fishing grounds, around the island were much appreciated, as were many smaller species that could be obtained from shore. Fishermen, who were specialists, went out to fish in their canoes in the spring and summer. Because of the scarcity of wood, these canoes, which are said to have had outriggers on both sides, were made, at least in more recent times, of small planks adzed to a precise fit and sewn together with *hau* (hibiscus) fiber. Hooks were made of stone and of human bone, the only kind of large mammalian bone available, and a variety of nets were used. In later times at least a tapu against eating and fishing for tuna and other deep-sea fish from May through September was strongly enforced. Many islanders still believe that they will suffer from *mare,* or asthma, if they violate this prohibition.

These people had no pottery, nor was it the custom to boil food. The only water container was the gourd. The only cooking device was the earth oven, or *umu,* within which food was cooked with heated stones. This oven was similar to the Chilean *curanto.*

Dwellings were of several kinds. In the exposed lava flows of the island there are many caves of a great variety of forms and sizes. Some of these are volcanic tubes from which streams of molten lava flowed as the lava was cooling. Many are well protected and commodious natural shelters, not nearly so uncomfortable as people not familiar with them might think. Stone walls with doorways were built across their entrances and parts of the interiors were terraced to provide level living areas which were covered with grass or matting. In these tunnels lived not only the newly arrived people of Hotu Matu'a but also later generations.

Many people also built houses in a very distinctive local style. I mentioned earlier the master builder Nuku Kehu who made the first of these houses at Anakena for Hotu Matu'a. This local style is called hare paenga. Elongated squared blocks of basalt of large size were carved and precisely fitted together to form a narrow elliptical foundation. Cylindrical holes several inches in diameter and depth were pecked into the upper surfaces of these to receive the superstructure poles. These latter were bent together to form a roof ridge and, with a series of horizontal elements added, were lashed to form a framework that was covered with thatch. The entrances were small lateral crawlways, and there were no windows. The finished structure resembled nothing so much as a large over-turned canoe. Along the entrance side was usually placed a crescent-shaped pavement of large, rounded beach boulders. Sometimes small stone statues were placed at either side of the door. Some such houses were made without basalt foundations, the ends of their framework poles being buried directly in the ground. They were dark inside and were used principally for sleeping, as these people did their cooking outside and lived outdoor lives.

Perhaps the canoelike form of these houses was a reflection of the deep-seated marine mentality of the islanders. Since they gave the name "boats of bones" (*naka ivi*) to the long narrow masonry structures that were the sepulchers of the dead, one gets the impression that neither in life nor death did they separate themselves from the symbolism of seafaring.

Clothing was scanty and difficult to procure. Most was made of the bark of the paper mulberry, or *mahute* (*Broussonetia papyrifera*), presumably also imported by the colonists. This is a small tree which does not grow as well on Easter Island as on many other Polynesian islands. It had to be protected from the wind by special small masonry enclosures of cylindrical shape, called *manavai*. These are still frequently to be seen, sometimes in large clusters, around the ruins of the old households. The bark was not woven but was pounded into thin, flat sheets that were sewn and quilted together with thread made of hau fiber and eyed needles of bone.

This material was made into loincloths and a kind of cape that was worn hanging from the shoulders and served at night as a sleeping cover.

The early European accounts suggest that the islanders were obsessed with hats. A variety of local forms called *ha'u* were made. Some were conical in shape, while others were bands or diadems of mahute adorned with multicolored chicken feathers. The use of the various ha'u reflected the nature of festive occasions, the rank of the person, and the emotional state of the wearer. To cite a single example, the *ha'u teketeke* was unique in having two long plumes in front. When a man was infuriated by some offense by another person he wore the ha'u teketeke in reverse with two plumes hanging behind. This was a serious symbolic manifestation of intentions of aggression and vengeance.

It is not surprising that a people who placed such value on head coverings should be enchanted when they first saw the hats of the Europeans who arrived in the eighteenth century. The newcomers found that the problem of keeping possession of their hats was a serious one indeed, for the islanders could not resist the temptation to appropriate any that they could snatch or entice away from their owners. La Pérouse relates that he and almost all who accompanied him on a stroll across the island returned to the ship hatless.[6] At the foot of the hill called Puha near the road to Vaitea is a place traditionally known by the name of Ko te hikonga ha'u o Miti Rangi a Ika Uri, which means "the place at which Ika Uri stole the hat of Miti Rangi." Undoubtedly these last two words are a local version of the title Mister and some English name. Very probably one of the men with Captain Cook, who were the only English-speaking people to have been on Easter Island in the eighteenth century, was the one to lose his hat here.

In this tiny scrap of parenthetical information we see an act and a commemoration as typical as it is symbolic. The islanders were

A moai kavakava ("statue with ribs") collected from Easter Island before 1833; about one-half actual size (Peabody Museum, Harvard University)

prone to apply names to minute localities, and a great many of these names are used even now. On such an isolated island, where great events were few and life was monotonous, the commemoration of such an insignificant incident is not at all unusual.

Materials for making tools and weapons were not available in great variety. Though wood undoubtedly was plentiful in earlier times, it gradually became scarce. Shortly after European contact it had apparently become so short in supply that even the small fishing canoes that were seen in use by the earliest visitors could no longer be made. However, excellent sculpture in wood was made in great variety up to modern times. Among the forms are the crescent-shaped *rei miro* worn as pectorals by the ariki; dance paddles; lizards called *moko*, which were sometimes placed at the entrances of houses; insignia of rank made in the form of clubs and called *ao*; and many others. The most typical wooden statues seen today are the *moai kavakava* (statue with ribs). These have the appearance of desiccated corpses with protruding ribs and sunken abdomens and are said to represent spirits, or *akuaku*. They are said to have been carved first by Tu'u ko Iho, who may have been the husband of Ava Rei Pua, sister of Hotu Matu'a. The legend told to me relates that he saw such spirits when walking alone and later made carvings of them. He made the figures move like puppets with strings and exhibited them in his house, which became known as *ko te hare hakahaere moai*, or "house in which the statues are made to walk." I shall have more to say about akuaku later.

Two kinds of stone useful for tools were found in abundance on Easter Island. These were obsidian; which provided glass-like cutting edges, and a tough, fine-grained basalt which could be ground and polished to precise contours. Of this last material, incredible as it may sound, beautiful polished fish hooks were made. These have not been found on other islands and are works of art as well as practical tools. The basalt was most frequently used for adzes, of which some were precisely formed and polished to fine edges excellent for wood cutting. Other rougher examples were used for stone cutting. Obsidian served to provide a great variety of cutting and scraping tools, drills, and files. It was available in tremendous quantities at a quarry at Maunga Orito in the southwest part of the island. This excellent volcanic glass is rarely found on Pacific islands.

Bone, so important to people who know no metals, posed a difficult problem. Bones of fish and birds were available, but the only large mammal bones were those of humans. These were frequently used, especially for beautifully made and polished fish hooks smaller than those of stone. Eyed needles for sewing the mahute were made of fish and bird bones. A noteworthy instrument of bone called *iuhi tatu* was used for tattooing. This is a slender needle ending in a line of three or four points so tiny and perfectly formed that it is difficult to understand how they were produced. These were daubed with soot and driven into the skin to form permanent designs.

FIVE

Religious and Social Practices

IN MOST CULTURES, RELIGIOUS IDEAS AND CUSTOMS OCCUPY A HIGH PLACE among the values. Unfortunately, relatively little is known about the Easter Island forms of these, and few memories have been preserved in the traditions. Just before and after the arrival of the first Europeans the islanders suffered from serious internally and externally caused catastrophes which eventually resulted in almost total destruction of the population, including most of the priesthood and others who possessed esoteric knowledge. This appears to be the greatest single factor responsible for the lack of memories of the old religion, as well as of many other social customs.

The little information that exists suggests clearly that the people of Easter Island had a religion related in many aspects to that of other Polynesian islands, of which more complete accounts of the cosmology are available and much more is known about concepts of supernatural power, deities, and divine personalities. The typically Polynesian notions of mana and tapu have already been discussed, and there is no doubt that these were fundamental in the religious life of the island.

Not all of the deities widely encountered in Polynesia appear to have been known on Easter Island, though some were, and one is said to have perished on these shores. This was Tangaroa, who for the Maori of New Zealand and the people of the Marquesas was the god of wind, of the sea, and of fishing, and for the people of Samoa and Tonga the first builder of houses and boats and the god of craftsmen. Without doubt he was an ancestor regarded as divine. According to local tradition he met a tragic end on Easter Island. In the form of a sea lion, called *pakia* here, he arrived at a small inlet near Hotu Iti which still bears the name of Hanga Tangaroa Mea, or Bay of the Red Tangaroa. Some people saw the sea lion on the beach. Regarding it as a good food source, they bound it with ropes and beat it with clubs. Tangaroa cried out desperately, "I am an ariki. I am Tangaroa. Let me go." His words were useless. They did not believe him, calling him *pakia re'o-o*, lying sea lion. He was killed without pity because the islanders wanted to cook him in an umu and eat him. The meat did not cook well and remained *re'e*, or half raw and red in color. They sent a present of some of it to friends on the other side of the island. They also could not cook it, and the place where they tried is called Re'e to this day. Thus the great Tangaroa, who was celebrated and deified in other parts of Polynesia, ignominiously ended his days as a victim of the voracity of people who did not understand what they were doing.

The name of the widely known Polynesian god Hiro survives on Easter Island in an old chant recited to produce rain and in several place names. As I mentioned earlier, the two landing points of Hotu Matu'a's party at Anakena were called Hiro Moko and Hanga o Hiro. We know nothing about the powers and characteristics of this god as he was known on Easter Island.

Of personalities that appear to have been regarded as true gods on the island only one stands out with any clarity. This is the creator Makemake. It is strange that he figures only in Easter Island mythology and is not known by this name in any other part of Polynesia. Métraux thinks that Makemake is the local Easter Island name for the god generally known in Polynesia as Tane.[1] Possibly this is true.

A very interesting scrap of information about Makemake is

found among the reports of the González expedition which visited the island in 1770. In a religious procession the Spaniards carried three crosses to the summits of three small hills on the slopes of the volcano Poike and placed them there. The islanders understood that a religious ceremony was being carried out and contributed to it by filling the air with cries to Makemake.[2] Mean what it may, in the small island museum there is a stone found on the heights of Poike which bears three incised crosses. Perhaps these were carved by an islander as a souvenir of the event.

Arturo Teao had heard from old people the story of how Makemake had created the world. This is his version.

"Makemake was alone. This was not good. Makemake took a gourd of water and looked inside. The shadow of Makemake entered the water. Makemake saw how the shadow of his face had entered the water. Makemake greeted his own shadow saying, 'Bless you, young man. How handsome you are. You look like me.' A bird alighted suddenly on the right shoulder of Makemake. Seeing that it was a being with a beak, wings, and feathers he was startled. He took the shadow and the bird and placed them together.

"Later Makemake thought about creating a man who would be the same as himself and who would talk and converse.

"Makemake with his semen fertilized a stone. There was no result. It was a thing badly made.

"He fertilized water. The result was a failure. There were born only the little fish called *paroko*.

"He fertilized red earth. From this man was born. Makemake saw that he was well made."

This version may have been influenced to some extent by Christian ideas. The story in its essentials probably does not have Christian inspiration, however, because the text includes many words now long obsolete in the modern form of the local language.

Much better remembered today than the gods are beliefs in the supernatural spirits called akuaku who were thought to come to the island or to reside in various parts of it. I was told the story of a certain islander called Moa Para who was carried away to the islet of Sala y Gómez by an akuaku called Haua a Motu Motiro Hiva. There he found no vegetable food and could obtain only fish to eat. When he became unhappy and desired to return to his native island, Haua appeared again and, sympathetic to his nostalgia, called a turtle and commanded it to carry him home.

Not all akuaku were characterized by benevolence toward people, but there were two who were outstandingly well disposed—Tare and his inseparable companion Rapahango. I was told that one day they visited a man who lived near a rock called Puku u'i Atua, "the rock of the vision of the spirit." This man, who was without a wife, begged them to go and find a certain woman who had been left in Hiva and bring her to him. He promised that he would not become a jealous husband or treat her badly, and they complied with his wish. For a time the couple lived happily, but one day the woman went to the house of another man to borrow fire. When she did not come back immediately, her husband became suspicious, and when she returned he beat her severely. She fled as fast as she could and eventually reached a small islet called Motu Takataka which lies off the shore of Poike. The man pursued her to take her back to his house, but at the moment of his arrival a rainbow appeared. The woman entered into the rainbow and returned to Hiva. The wife of the jealous man was lost to him forever.

It is said that Tare and Rapahango were accustomed to appear at night at houses where tuna was being cooked in earth ovens. They would call from the darkness to the owner of the house and beg a piece of fish, not for themselves, but to carry to another house where there was no food.

Many akuaku were thought to live in specific localities and were known by name. Mrs. Routledge collected a list of ninety with their places of residence.[3] The names of only a few are remembered today. Many aided the people of the kin-groups in their localities and were hostile to intruders. Sometimes they punished people severely. A story is told of one Vaka Tuku Onge who lived near

Mahatua, and who went one night with a companion to hunt makohe birds in territory that belonged to another group. The method of hunting was to catch the birds with the hands while they were roosting. He caught ten and gave them to his companion. When he returned to catch another, an akuaku entered into the bird, and it flapped its wings and flew away. Then several akuaku in human form appeared and began to beat him. They continued until the spirit of one of his ancestors, called Moaha, rescued him and led him by the hand to the house of his father Teatea. There he remained for a month, bleeding at the mouth and nose. His father explained to him that the fault was his. He should not have hunted birds in another group's territory. For violating this tapu he had been punished by the akuaku.

Certain former customs that may have been religious in origin or at least have had religious overtones involved reverence for beauty. These were practices which had the object of preserving the fair complexions of boys and girls. Light skin color was much admired, and the traditions agree with the testimony of the early European explorers that there were many people of very fair complexion, just as there are today. Behrens in 1722 mentions this. He wrote: "As for their complection they are brownish, about the hue of a Spaniard, yet one finds some among them of a darker shade and others quite white."[4] Brother Eugène, who lived on Easter Island during nine months of 1864, wrote. "Their color even though somewhat coppery, differs only a little from that of Europeans, and many of them even are entirely white."[5]

As the islanders wore little clothing and lived most of their lives in the open, they tanned easily to a copper color. In their desire to conserve the beautiful white skin of some of their children (*poki*) they selected the most beautiful among them and required them to stay inside the houses (*huru hare*). The *poki huru hare* were permitted to go out very little, so they would not lose their white skin color. These young victims of the beauty concepts of their elders would seem to have spent rather sad and monotonous childhoods.

When they reached adolescence they were exhibited to the public in certain dances called *hikinga kaunga*. Long, narrow pathways were prepared and paved with smooth stones. Some of these may still be seen. On these the boys and girls, wearing very little clothing, and with their faces painted with red and yellow pigment, sang and danced. Spectators arranged themselves on either side of the pathway.

Probably related to this in some way was the seclusion of the *neru*. In the steep cliffs at the foot of the east slope of Poike are two caves called Ana o Keke and Ana More Mata Puku, in which lived especially chosen young people of both sexes, called *neru*, who were secluded in these caves to conserve their white complexions. They are said to have remained celibate and to have allowed their hair and fingernails to grow.

Beauty was also enhanced by much body painting and tatooing. Earths of various colors were used. Among the men were some who painted themselves with charcoal. González saw men thus painted and remarked that in spite of this they looked more like Europeans than American Indians.[6] The cosmetic preferred by the women was *kiea*, a red-colored earth containing much hematite. This was to be found in a certain locality in the region of Poike. They mixed it with the fragrant juice of the sandalwood tree and formed it into little balls. With these they painted themselves before going out to dances and ceremonies, just as women today use rouge and lipstick.

A legend is told of a certain Ure Pooi, who, much like younger brothers in many other parts of the world, played a trick on the vain young girls of his family, who had been making careful preparations to go to a ceremony in a distant part of the island. Before going to bed on the night before the ceremony they prepared their little balls of kiea and placed them in readiness. Ure Pooi rose in the middle of the night and stealthily crept to some nearby trees on which chickens were roosting. He struck his buttocks with his palms in imitation of awakening roosters. At this sound all the chickens in the vicinity began to shake themselves and cry out. The young girls, thinking dawn was about to break, arose, painted their faces, and set out for the dance. They arrived far too early and had to sit waiting for several hours, while the kiea ran from their faces. The girls had to borrow more paint and listen to the laughter of Ure Pooi.

Tattooing was also of great importance. It was done by experts under the supervision of the ariki henua. A small bone punch with several very tiny comblike prongs on the end was dipped in black pigment made of burned ti leaves and driven into the skin. It was a painful and lengthy process, repeated at various times during an individual's life. Designs in great variety were made on all parts of the body, and the work was excellent. We know little about the social significance of the tattooing or the symbolic value of the designs.

As in all Polynesia, interest in dances and other ceremonies was well developed. An important class of such ceremonies was called *koro*. This included all the ceremonies that were celebrated with series of songs and with feasting. They were apparently given in honor of a deceased person or in memory of some important event. There were many kinds, and they were attended by large audiences. Some were rather unusual in character. Two examples will illustrate what I mean.

One frequent koro was the *paina*. It was given by a son with the object of honoring both the memory of his dead father and a good friend of his father who had helped him in times of scarcity of food or provided aid in time of war. The ceremony was essentially a public testimonial of gratitude to both. The son first raised a figure made on a wooden frame about 10 feet in height and covered it with mahute cloth. At its top was a head with an open mouth. The figure was erected in the vicinity of the ahu where the father was buried and was surrounded by a stone circle. The Spanish saw one of these figures in 1770 and said that it resembled the figures of

Judas that were burned in Spain during Holy Week.[7] When the people had assembled, the organizer of the ceremony crawled into the figure and through its mouth, in a sad voice, cried out his memories of his father and gave thanks to his father's friend. The ceremony ended in a great feast provided by the organizer for all present. Many chickens were distributed, as well as food of other kinds.

Another unique Easter Island ceremony was that of the *miro oone*, or boat of earth. An elongated mound of earth was heaped up in the form of a canoe. The remains of several of these may be seen today. A group representing the captain and crew seated themselves in this. Few of the details of the ceremony that followed are remembered, but it involved innumerable songs and much feasting. Whether or not this commemorated the voyage of Hotu Matu'a and his people is not known, but it was another typical manifestation of the marine mentality of the islanders.

The stone foundation of a boat-shaped house (haere paenga);
this style of building may also reflect the marine orientation
of the Easter Islanders

SIX

The Inscribed Tablets

MUCH THAT IS SADLY EXAGGERATED HAS BEEN WRITTEN FOR POPULAR consumption about Easter Island. One may read stories of sunken continents and of statues being blown from the quarries to the ahu by volcanic eruptions. Authors who knew little about what they wrote have created all sorts of mysteries where none really exist. Their exaggerations and misinformation have made esoteric and incomprehensible much that has a reasonable and moderate explanation. But one remarkable product of the old culture is still enveloped in true clouds of mystery and may remain so forever. This is the Easter Island script. Written languages, wherever found, are almost always the product of large societies and complicated cultures which have great masses of information that require recording. They result from this need and are indeed unusual as products of small and isolated groups. That a script would be needed or invented by the tiny community of Easter Island is genuinely astonishing. Yet no source away from the island from which this script could have been derived has yet been identified.

The first European to become aware of this script was the missionary Brother Eugène Eyraud, who, in his account of his nine months' residence on the island in 1864, wrote:

"In all the houses are encountered tablets or staffs of wood covered with hieroglyphics. These are figures of animals unknown in the island which the people inscribed with sharp stones. Each figure has its name but the little account that they take of these tablets inclines me to believe that these characters, the remains of primitive writing, are for them today, a usage which they preserved without inquiry into their meaning."[1]

Brother Eugène seems to have been mistaken when he spoke of figures of animals unknown on the island, but his impression that at the time of his visit the understanding of the characters had been almost completely lost was probably quite correct. Thanks to his information and that of the other early missionaries, systematic scholars became interested almost immediately in this enigmatic script. One of the first of these was Tepano Jaussen, then Bishop of Tahiti.

The old and complete name of the tablets was *ko hau motu mo rongorongo*, which, literally translated, means "lines of script for recitation." Usually one hears the abbreviated form *ko hau rongorongo*, or "lines for recitation." According to the tradition, Hotu Matu'a brought with him from Hiva sixty-seven of these inscribed tablets. With him came also scholars who knew the art of writing and reciting the inscriptions. They bore the title of *maori ko hau rongorongo*, *maori* being the honorific title used by masters of any craft.

Most of the tablets are somewhat irregular, flat, wooden boards with rounded edges, about 12 to 20 inches long. They are completely covered with neat rows of tiny, beautifully incised symbols, each generally from 3/8 to 5/8 of an inch long. The symbols include a fascinating multitude of little figures of men in a variety of positions, flying birds, animals, what appear to be plants, celestial objects, and geometrical forms. They are complex in detail yet at the same time drawn with calligraphic flow. There are hundreds of different signs—far too many to suggest any sort of phonetic alphabet or syllabary. The sequence of the writing is a rare and curious one called "reversed boustrophedon"—that is, each line

Easter Island script on a section of a rongorongo tablet in the National Museum of Natural History, Santiago de Chile

of script when it reaches the edge of the board turns back upside down to form the next line. This means that to read the script one must turn the board around at the end of each line. There is no doubt that this writing was inscribed by experts and that it represents a work of art as well as a script.

I imagine that with the same care with which Vakai a Heva brought her newborn child Tu'u Maheke from the canoe to the shore, Hotu Matu'a carried to the new land his precious and sacred tablets. If in this historic moment he had had a prophetic vision of the future, he would have brought together his maori ko hau rongorongo, and the anguished Polynesian cry of despair, *aue! aue!*, would have filled the air. "Our ko hau rongorongo are lost! Future events will destroy these sacred tablets which we bring with us and those which we will make in our new land. Men of other races will guard a few that remain as priceless objects, and their maori will study them in vain without being able to read them. Our ko hau motu mo rongorongo will be lost forever. Aue! Aue!"

These words that I have placed in the mouth of Hotu Matu'a may seem too pessimistic to more than one of the linguists now dedicated to the decipherment of the tablets. Only the future will show which opinion is justified.

According to the scarce information which tradition has preserved there were at least three separate classes of inscriptions. The *ko hau kiri taku ki te atua* recorded hymns in honor of Makemake and other divine personalities. The *ko hau ta'u* recorded crimes or other deeds of individuals. The *ko hau ika* were dedicated to the memory of those who fell in wars or other conflicts. It is said that tablets bearing genealogical records also existed, but we know even less about these. Since Brother Eugène said that he saw tablets in all the houses he visited and that others were kept in caves, the total number must have been considerable. It is not unlikely that in his time several thousand existed.

Apparently the guarding of the tablets and the maintenance of the art of writing them were under the direct control of the ariki henua, of which the first was Hotu Matu'a. To aid him he had the services of the maori rongorongo. There were organized schools for teaching the art of writing, and the students presented themselves with their teachers for annual examination at Anakena.

An old man who in his youth had attended one of these schools, located near Ahu Akapu on the west coast, told several islanders to whom I talked something of what went on there. The discipline was very strict. Students were not permitted to talk or to play but were required to kneel and sit on their heels with their hands folded together across their chests and to pay strict attention. They were beaten if their minds wandered. It is probable that a tablet bearing a hymn to Makemake was used as a text. After learning to recite, the students began to copy the characters to accustom themselves to writing. These copying exercises were not done on wood, but on banana leaves with a stylus of bone or wood. Later the students wrote on wooden tablets with sharp-pointed gravers made of obsidian or shark teeth.

Only a few tablets survive today.[2] Three excellent and well-preserved examples can be seen in the Museo Nacional de Historia Natural at the Quinta Normal in Santiago de Chile. The same museum also has a partly burned fragment on which the characters are still quite visible; this was found in 1937 close to the stone foundations of an ancient destroyed house near Hanga Hoonu, by the late José Pate, an islander who had a keen interest in the old ways. He gave it to me and I sent it to the Museo Nacional. In cities in the United States and Europe various museums have a total of twenty additional examples, of which three are poorly preserved and three others are small and have very few characters. The amount of text available to linguists is thus sharply limited, and in this fact lies one of the most serious obstacles to deciphering the script.

One of the important reasons for the loss of so many tablets lay in the superstitious fears of their owners. Very few dared to give or trade them to foreigners. The tapu by which they were protected involved serious prohibitions against allowing them to fall into alien hands. The fear of supernatural vengeance should they be taken away from the island was terrifying to most people. An old islander told me that many years ago an old man showed him an authentic tablet and exacted his strict promise not to reveal its existence. In spite of this precaution, the old man later burned the precious object so that he might rest assured that it would never leave the island.

Another cause of loss stemmed from the custom of keeping the sacred tablets in secret caves where they were decomposed by moisture. Juan Araki, an old islander who died in 1949, told me that one day an old man named Paoa Hitaki led him to a place high on the slopes of the volcano Rano Kau. The old man instructed Juan to remain near the summit and to prepare a sacred offering of food in an earth oven, while he descended and disappeared among some trees inside the crater. After several hours he returned, bearing in his hands a tablet in a good state of preservation. He said, "Seven of the ko hau rongorongo in the cave are decomposed. This is the only one in good condition."

Fear of tapu has diminished sufficiently in the minds of many islanders today that they would take tablets from caves to sell if they could find them, and some search for the entrances to such caves. The traditions tell that the openings of such caves were carefully blocked up and concealed by their owners, and very few that could be classified as such repositories have been found. No new ko hau rongorongo have been discovered recently, and it seems likely that any that might turn up in the future would be in too bad condition to be of much use.

A third agent of destruction was fire among the highly inflammable thatched houses. Both before and after the arrival of the first Europeans the island was ravaged by internal wars of which I shall speak later. Many houses were burned in these conflicts and with them the sacred tablets they contained. The tablet found by José Pate appears to have been an accidental survivor of such a conflagration.

Many attempts have been made to decipher the inscriptions. The first was made in Tahiti by Bishop Jaussen. He requested the group of missionaries who were sent to the island in 1866 to collect and send to him as many tablets as they could find. Even at this relatively early period they could acquire only three. These are today in the museum of The Congregation of the Sacred Hearts in Grottaferrata near Rome. In Tahiti Bishop Jaussen became acquainted with an Easter Islander named Metoro who lived there and who was said to be able to read the tablets. When asked to do so he complied, but the experiment was not satisfactory, since he appeared to be reciting memorized texts or simply describing the figures, rather than actually reading the inscribed characters. He may have learned by heart some texts inscribed on tablets without knowing how to read the characters.[3] Similar results were obtained later by others who consulted islanders with reputations as maori ko hau rongorongo. It appears that by this time the last of the truly literate maori were dead.

Among recent publications related to this problem are several of special interest. A Hungarian scholar, Guillaume de Hevesy, in 1932 called attention to apparent similarities between some of the ko hau rongorongo characters and some of the characters in a script discovered in a 3000-year-old civilization in the Indus Valley.[4] The publication was initially regarded as an important discovery with the implication that the people of Hotu Matu'a might have originated in that part of India. Specialists today are inclined to the opinion that the similarities are not close or frequent enough to suggest any contact between these two cultures so separated in space and time. They are more likely to be the sort of similarities that often exist between objects of independent origin in cultures which have no historical relationships.

The most complete work dealing with the problem up to the present time is *Grundlagen zur Entzifferung der Osterinselschrift* (Foundations for the Decipherment of the Easter Island Script) by Thomas Barthel, professor of ethnology at the University of Tübingen. He has presented detailed descriptions and photographs of all the tablets known, a complete enumeration of the characters and the location of each in the lines of the tablets, the texts of the recitations made by Metoro for Bishop Jaussen, and a commentary on the objects represented in the characters. This voluminous work is a true *Corpus Inscriptionum Paschalis Insulae*, but the translations it provides are not very intelligible.

A group of Russian scholars, including J. V. Knorozov, I. K. Fedorova, and A. M. Kondratov, have also spent some years studying the problem from a point of view rather different from that of Barthel. They too have not yet succeeded in producing a satisfactory translation.

That the ko hau rongorongo will ever be deciphered seems unlikely for several reasons. The characters appear to be ideographs, similar in principle to those of the Chinese script. There is no evidence that any of them is phonetic. This means that their relationship to the spoken language is to ideas rather than words and is an arbitrary one. The decipherment of one character offers no clue to the sound of the spoken word and provides relatively little aid in discovering the meaning of another character. The problem here is infinitely more difficult than it would be if a relatively small number of phonetic characters symbolized the sounds of a spoken language.

Our understanding of the old language of Easter Island, which the script undoubtedly represents, is by no means complete. This is especially true of archaic forms no longer used, the language of the old poetry, and obscure allusions to things, ideas, and events now unknown, which must have been abundant in the literature of the tablets. To obtain insights of this kind it would be necessary to call back from their tombs the long-dead maori. The speech of the modern islanders, while still a Polynesian language, has undergone considerable evolution and has received many loan words from Tahitian, Spanish, English, and other languages. It is very different from the language in which the script must have been written.

Furthermore, if some thousands of tablets had been preserved, instead of the pitifully few that survive, it might have been possible to carry out the kinds of comparative studies which are impossible with the tiny available remnants.

Though their meaning remains unknown to us, the tablets themselves still stand as a unique monument to the cultural sophistication of this tiny and isolated community that is far more important than the largest of the stone statues at Rano Raraku.

SEVEN

The Death of Hotu Matu'a and the Coming of Other Immigrants

EASTER ISLAND TRADITION, AS I HAVE INDICATED, PROVIDES A GOOD DEAL OF information about Hotu Matu'a's arrival. However, for his later years the traditional information is scanty and fails to tell us many of the things we would like to know. If we had, and could read, the literature of the ko hau rongorongo perhaps much that is obscure would become clear. Even so, some items of interest have been remembered.

The tradition as I heard it relates that Hotu Matu'a lived for some years at Anakena in the house built by the master builder Nuku Kehu. As time passed, his life with Vakai a Heva became marred by discord. As seems true with most marital difficulties, the incident that caused their final separation was not one of great importance. One day Hotu Matu'a in a moment of bad humor became annoyed with the crying of his child Tu'u Maheke and scolded him. Vakai a Heva, who appears to have been a vigorous and strong-minded woman, sprang immediately to the defense of her child and insulted her husband. Hotu Matu'a became angry and aggrieved and left Anakena and his family. Vakai a Heva followed him after a time, but Hotu Matu'a wanted to see no more of her and moved to another place. The detailed tradition relates that she followed him to four separate places of residence. Each time he fled at her arrival. When she appeared for the fifth time at Akahanga she fell ill and died. She was buried there.

The tradition also tells that, after leaving Anakena, Hotu Matu'a led a solitary life and devoted himself to agricultural pursuits. As he was an ariki henua and a sacred person, he should have delegated such work to subordinates and offered only the stimulation of his good advice. He was apparently obsessed with the desire to provide a secure economic future for his people.

He was especially worried by the scarcity of water. As the island is without flowing streams today, water then also may have been a serious problem as numbers increased. Large quantities would have been available in the crater lakes of Rano Kau, Rano Raraku, and Rano Aroi, but these are localized and difficult of access. Then as today the island probably had a number of small water sources in pockets among the lava flows. Even so, water has been a most serious problem on the island in modern times. The nature of the soil is such that rain water, which is the only source, disappears quickly and emerges along the shore at or below sea level. Hotu Matu'a's concern led him to the discovery that shallow wells could be excavated on the extreme edge of the coast, which would produce water somewhat contaminated by the sea but still fit for human use. He had such wells dug at several points. With these he rejoiced in having solved a vital problem.

After years had passed he eventually fell mortally ill. He went to the heights of the volcano called Rano Kau and had his four sons called to him. The ariki henua looked at the first through his dimming eyes and said, "Who are you?"

His eldest son, who had been born at Anakena on the day of the arrival at Easter Island, answered, "It is I, Tu'u Maheke."

The old ariki blessed him by saying, "May good luck always accompany you, my eldest son. There is much sand in your land of Anakena. There are many insects in your land." He meant by this that the descendants of Tu'u Maheke in his territory of Anakena would become as numerous as the insects and the grains of sand.

His eldest son stepped back, and his second son, Miru te Mata

Nui, came forward. Hotu Matu'a said, "May good luck be with you. Take care of your people."

The third son appeared. Hotu Matu'a asked, "Who are you?"

The answer came. "I am Tu'u te Mata Nui, son of Hotu Matu'a."

The ruler said, "May good luck be with you. There are many round pebbles in Hanga Te Pau. There are many shells in Te Hue." Here again he was apparently predicting that the people of Tu'u te Mata Nui would become numerous.

Finally the youngest son entered. The old ariki asked, "Who are you?"

The youngest replied, "I am Hotu Iti te Mata Iti, son of Hotu Matu'a." The ariki put his arms around him and kissed him on both cheeks, for he knew that he was a good and strong son.

He said, "May good luck be with you, Mata Iti, son of Hotu Matu'a. The *niuhi tapaka'i* are to be found in Motu Toremo in Hiva and also in your territory." Niuhi is a kind of hard-fighting fish, probably the hammer-headed shark. Tapaka'i is a word which is unknown in the modern language. It would seem that the ariki was comparing his youngest son to the valiant niuhi, and pointing out that, as in Motu Toremo in Hiva, there were also niuhi in the seas of Hotu Iti, the territory assigned to him. Thus he divided the island among his sons.

Just before his death he sent a young man to bring him water from a certain well which he had dug at Huareva in a locality between Vaihu and Akahanga. He apparently did this, not because he was thirsty, but in order to taste, as his death drew near, the water from a source that had solved the last of the great problems of his people. Had he wanted only to quench his thirst, the water in the crater lake of Rano Kau was much closer.

When he felt that the end was near he dragged himself to the western edge of the crater of Rano Kau. Here at the top of a precipitous cliff he supported himself between two rocky points that are still pointed out. In the sea below he could see the islet of Motu Nui. He looked toward the northwest in the direction of his native land of Hiva and called to the spirits of that place. He cried out to the akuaku called Kuihi, Kuaha, Tongau, and Opakako. He begged them to make the rooster of Ariange—presumably a place in Hiva—crow once more. In answer there came the distant cry *"o'oa take heuheu,"* which is the way roosters crow in Hiva as well as on Easter Island. This was for him the signal of farewell, and he begged his sons to carry him to his house at Akahanga, where he soon died. Though the traditional description of the last hours of the ariki henua may seem fanciful, it includes a familiar note of very human sentiment—that of the dying man who at the last turns his thoughts to his far-off and fondly remembered native land.

The sons put the mortal remains of their father on a litter and sadly carried him to a spot near the Bay of Akahanga. Here they made for him a tomb of stones and earth. It was a simple sepulcher of unremarkable form, quite unlike the spectacular burial places made in later times in the great stone ahu which I describe in Chapter 8.

The tradition describes the concern of the sons about the protection of Hotu Matu'a's head. They covered the corpse with a heavy mantle of sand in which they mixed many razor-edged flakes of obsidian which would cut the hands of those who came to rob. I mentioned earlier the strong belief in the sacredness of the head of a member of the royal family, as encountered by Father Roussel when he wanted to cut the hair of Ro Koroko te Tau. The belief in the sacredness of and magic power in the head of royal persons is widely found among Polynesians. The skulls of the dead ariki were considered objects of great value and thought to possess supernatural power of benefit to the possessor. Such skulls could be recognized by the incised symbols on the frontal bone. The happy possessor of such a skull guarded it carefully in the hope that its power would increase his agricultural yield and especially his flock of chickens. The skulls of royal persons were thus frequently stolen and the sons of Hotu Matu'a hoped to prevent this.

A tomb said to be that of Hotu Matu'a still exists. In the course of conservation work proposed for future years this tomb will probably be investigated and restored. Perhaps the sand and the obsidian flakes will be found as the tradition describes them. It might then be reasonable to place here a plaque commemorating the work of colonization of the great ariki henua.

Unfortunately it will not be possible to add to the plaque one item of information which we would like very much to have and which would be of the greatest importance to our knowledge of the history of the island. That is the date of Hotu Matu'a's death, from which the approximate time of the Polynesian immigration could be calculated.

It is truly lamentable that tradition has not preserved a definitive list of ariki henua from Hotu Matu'a to Kai Makoi and his son Maurata, who in 1862 were carried away by slavers, and, together with many other islanders, died on the Chincha Islands off the coast of Peru. If we had a surely authentic list of the succession of ariki, we could make an approximate calculation of the time of the colonization. But instead of one of which we can be sure, six lists have been recorded, and all are different. One was obtained by William J. Thomson who visited the island in 1886. Alexander P. Salmon, of European and Tahitian parentage, who was then on the island and was familiar with its tradition, was his informant. This list included fifty-seven names.[1] Two other lists were collected before Thomson's time. One, obtained by Father Roussel, included twenty-three names.[2] Another, collected by Bishop Jaussen, included thirty-one.[3] In 1914 Mrs. Routledge obtained two independent lists, each including thirty names, which have never been published and are not available to us.[4] A list recorded by Métraux in 1934 also included thirty names[5] (see Appendix II). Thus most of the evidence suggests a number around thirty. All the lists may well have included names of ariki who were not ariki henua. I agree with Métraux that the true number was probably between twenty and thirty. If we take into account the fact that the ariki henua customarily transferred their power during their lifetimes to their eldest sons, and consider fifteen years to be the average duration of a reign, the inconclusive evidence suggests that Hotu Matu'a probably arrived in the sixteenth century.

Until the second third of the twentieth century, Easter Island with its forbidding rockbound coasts and its dry and windswept grasslands was almost ignored by the outside world. Even in continental Chile it was considered of value only for raising sheep and as a place of exile for politicians. Recently, however, a great change has occurred. The island's hundreds of gigantic stone statues and impressive outdoor altars have captured the imagination of the world, and the island is becoming recognized as the most spectacular museum of prehistoric Polynesian art and architecture in the whole Pacific.

These noteworthy accomplishments, however, do not appear to have been conceived by the colonists brought by Hotu Matu'a, but at a later time, stimulated principally by another group of immigrants known as the Hanau Eepe.

The traditions describing the circumstances under which these later arrivals appeared vary somewhat in details. I am inclined to have greatest confidence in the story as told to me by Arturo Teao, who lived in the leprosarium. I recorded his version in May of 1936.

His version states that the new people appeared some time after the colonists of Hotu Matu'a were well established, and certain facts fit well with his account.

Hotu Matu'a's people are said to have given the new arrivals the name Hanau Eepe, or more correctly Tangata Hanau Eepe (broad or heavy-set men). In later times the people of Hotu Matu'a by contrast

Father Sebastian pointing out details
of an unfinished moai at the Rano Raraku quarry

The Death of Hotu Matu'a   89

*A partially
buried moai
and the central
platform
of Ahu Tahira at Vinapu*

After the moai had fallen, ahu were sometimes used for human burials

called themselves Hanau Momoko. Today the word momoko is a form of duplication of moko (lizard), which carries the sense of "sharp-pointed." The word then probably expressed the idea of something slender. Thus Hanau Momoko would mean "slender people."

To the surprise which the Hanau Momoko felt when they saw canoes bearing heavy-set men who appeared different from themselves was added their wonder at noting that the newcomers had ears pierced and greatly distended for the insertion of large ornaments. This fact has led to a curious confusion about the name Hanau Eepe. Various authors have asserted that the name means "long ears" and refers to these extended lobes. This erroneous translation resulted from the fortuitous phonetic similarity between the words *eepe*, which means "heavy-set," and *epe*, which means "ear lobe." There is no doubt that the name given to the newcomers actually means "heavy-set men," even though they also had *epe roroa*, or elongated ear lobes.

A great battle between these two groups, which I shall presently describe, resulted in the almost complete extermination of the Hanau Eepe. Their custom of enlarging the ear lobes was not lost, however. It was evidently taken over by the Hanau Momoko and survived into historic times; such ears were seen by the earlier visitors to the island. Brother Eugène describes the custom which in his time appears to have been practiced only by women. He said that when they were very young they pierced their ear lobes with a conical wooden awl. This they gradually pressed more deeply as the perforation increased in size. Later a roll of tree bark was introduced which acted as a spring and continued to dilate the opening. Eventually the lobes of the ear were converted into slender cords which rested on the shoulders.[6]

The Hanau Eepe immigrants are described as having included only men. This suggests that theirs was not a planned colonizing voyage like that of Hotu Matu'a. Thus they could well have been few in number. They took wives from among the local women, and thus their descendants possessed Hanau Momoko heredity, but these appear to have remained a distinct group.

Another detail of the tradition which seems significant also comes out in the context of the previously mentioned battle. The Hanau Eepe appear to have spoken a language different from that of the people of Hotu Matu'a. The tradition describes a defeated Hanau Eepe warrior who took refuge in a cave and when pricked by the lances of the Hanau Momoko cried out, "*Orro, orro, orro.*" This sounded strange to his captors because the double "r" sound did not exist in their language.

It would seem reasonable that some influence of the language of the Hanau Eepe might have remained in the modern speech, even though children commonly learn the language of their mothers. Perhaps some of the synonyms in use today might be so explained. However, none can unequivocally be demonstrated to be foreign to the basic structures of the surviving language. An interesting historical note may bear on this question. One of the members of the party of Gonzalez, in 1770, attempted to learn some words of the local language. By means of signs he elicited ninety-four words which he wrote down. Most words are clearly recognizable today as those of the local language, but the curious fact that commands attention is that the words recorded for the numerals from one to ten are totally different from any known to have been used on the island.[7] That some confusion of translation was involved seems unlikely, for these ten words have no known meaning whatever in the local speech. Perhaps this series of numerals belonged to the language of the Hanau Eepe. If the language to which these ten numerals belong could be discovered, the information would be of great interest, for we today echo the same question asked by the Hanau Momoko: Whence came these people?

In all Polynesia, only in the Marquesas was the custom of dilating ear lobes practiced. It is also noteworthy that a similar custom was practiced in prehistoric Peru. Peter Buck stated his opinion that one of the migrations to Easter Island came from the Marquesas and perhaps the Hanau Eepe reached Easter Island from there.[8] Originally the practice of distending the ear lobes may have come from Peru, as Heyerdahl suggests.[9] This is a speculation which we cannot support with evidence, but I am inclined to think it probable, for according to tradition it was the Hanau Eepe who brought to the island the idea of building the great masonry ahu, or altars. The most perfect of these, in the locality of Vinapu, has precisely fitted large blocks highly reminiscent of some of the prehistoric masonry of Peru.

The traditions seem to suggest that these gigantic outdoor altars did not exist in Hotu Matu'a's time. Credit for the beginning of this spectacular activity is traditionally given to the Hanau Eepe. It was they who built the first of the great ahu, and, seeing their work, the Hanau Momoko were stimulated to follow their example. According to legend, however, the Hanau Momoko first carved the stone of Rano Raraku into images representative of dead ancestors and placed these on ahu, and the Hanau Eepe in turn followed their example. The island eventually became dotted with great altars bearing spectacular statues.

EIGHT

The Outdoor Altars

FROM THE ARCHITECTURAL INTEREST AND THE STATUE-CARVING ACTIVITY which appears to have been stimulated by it, there developed on the island a religious building obsession of high intensity. The great numbers of gigantic stone statues and impressive masonry monuments are remarkable evidence of the ingenuity and industry of the island people. Even though larger and more numerous statues and religious structures have been produced by prehistoric peoples in other parts of the world, those of Easter Island seem to command unusual attention and fire the imagination of the visitor—perhaps because they are found on an island so far from the stimulation of the larger culture centers of the world. The words of Mrs. Scoresby Routledge, written during her sixteen-month residence in 1914 and 1915, express a widely felt reaction. "In Easter Island the past is the present, it is impossible to escape from it; the inhabitants of to-day are less real than the men who have gone; the shadows of the departed builders still possess the land. Voluntarily or involuntarily the sojourner must hold commune with those old workers; for the whole air vibrates with a vast purpose and energy which has been and is no more. What was it? Why was it?"[1]

The commonest local religious structure, the ahu, is a form of the eastern Polynesian *marae*. The ahu do not appear to have been expressions of a religious cult organized on an island-wide basis, but the property of the local kin-groups that owned the territory where they were located. There are more than 245 ahu, most of which form an almost unbroken line along the coasts except for the areas of high cliffs around Poike and Rano Kau, though some occupy cliff-edge sites in other places. They tend to be concentrated around good landing places and areas especially favorable for habitation. A few occupy interior sites. Some are clearly unfinished, and many have been rebuilt and altered several times with significant changes in their architectural details. The ravages of prehistoric local conflicts have destroyed most to the point that the ruins must be studied carefully to determine what the original characteristics really were.

There are several varieties of these structures, and all of the styles were probably not built at the same time. Some appear to be essentially gigantic altars where religious ceremonies must have been carried out. Others seem to have been constructed primarily for purposes of burial or cremation. Sometimes the architectural characteristics are mixed, suggesting that the emphasis may have been changed at different periods.

The most spectacular variant is the *ahu moai*, or ahu on which statues were placed. Though each of these has its distinctive individuality and as a group they reveal wide variation, their typical form can be described in broad general terms. The most constant feature is a narrow flat-topped platform most commonly located near to and parallel to the shore. Some of these approach 200 yards in length, and there are examples as much as 25 feet high. The usual breadth is from 6 to 15 feet. The walls of these platforms are most frequently made of large stones, sometimes precisely cut and fitted blocks, while the interiors are rubble. Facing stones may be horizontally laid blocks or gigantic vertical slabs. Sometimes inside the rubble of the platforms are found whole or fragmentary statues that may have surmounted earlier structures. No one knows why they were so concealed. Possibly they were thought to serve to transfer mana from an earlier ahu to a later one. Some platforms have elevated central sections, into which are set enormous flat stone pedestals for the placement of statues. These are typically flanked by lower lateral wings. Usually gently sloping ramps paved in various ways are built against the landward sides of the platforms. In some cases pavements are made of closely placed slabs or irregular stones, but the most beautiful and distinctive variety consists of parallel rows of large rounded beach boulders, set apart and with the intervening spaces filled with smoothly rounded beach pebbles.

Adjacent to the ramps there are usually large plazas which may be artificially flattened or naturally more or less level terrain. In a few cases these are outlined by earth embankments forming rectangular or irregular enclosures. Occasionally built on the plazas are small, rectangular masonry platforms that suggest altars. Large circles of stones are also seen; these are said to be foundations for the tapa-covered paina figures used in one of the kinds of koro ceremonies which I mentioned earlier. Sometimes inland of the plazas are boat-shaped thatched houses, usually placed in rows and said to have been occupied by members of the priesthood that served the ahu. The whole complex has the appearance of a gigantic open-air altar.

Little is known about the ceremonies formerly associated with these structures. The statues that rested on them are reported to have represented ancestors of the kin group owning the ahu and to have possessed supernatural power. It thus seems likely that the ceremonies contributed to a kin-group ancestor cult. At least in later times cadavers were placed on wooden platforms in front of the statues and left to dry. They were then removed to stone-lined tombs excavated into the ahu ramps and platforms. After the ahu were destroyed in warfare and the statues overthrown, many were extensively used for what appear to have been more casual inhumations. Cadavers were placed under and around the fallen statues and on other parts of ramps and covered with stones. This practice was so extensive that many ahu moai eventually became almost completely covered with disorderly piles of stones. In earlier times some cadavers appear to have been cremated in rectangular stone cysts located on the sea side of the central platforms. Whether these cremated cadavers were the deceased of the kin-group owning the ahu or the remains of victims of human sacrifice is not known. Traditions relate that human sacrifice by burning was sometimes practiced.

There are fifteen ahu moai which are of truly great dimensions and extraordinary artistic and architectural value. Sixteen others are somewhat smaller and less perfectly constructed. Seventeen have relatively low platforms, and fifty-two others, some of which are quite large, do not have distinctly separated ramp and platform. Whether these latter examples represent decadent forms, early prototypes, or simply style variants is not known.

Two ahu are especially noteworthy. One is located at a place called Vinapu near the west end of the south coast. Here, clustered in a kind of ceremonial center similar to others on the island, are three large ahu. The most unusual of these was probably called Ahu Tahira. It is by no means the largest of the ahu, but it is the most perfect of them all. The enormous squared and somewhat irregularly horizontally placed basalt blocks with which its platform and wings are faced are so perfectly fitted that the blade of a knife can hardly be passed between them. Though the stones tend to be coursed, each great stone is fitted to its neighbor individually so that no two are exactly alike. This is a remarkable example of cut-and-try craftsmanship in which stones weighing many tons were repeatedly placed against each other and their adjoining surfaces gradually reduced by pecking until they abutted precisely. The wall surfaces bulge slightly between the joints, and the whole is reminiscent of the finest Inca masonry. Ahu Tahira is the best example of a type of masonry seen in a somewhat less perfect form in many other ahu. The sloping ramp is paved with rows of very large rounded beach boulders with the spaces between filled with smooth beach pebbles. As measured by engineering problems involved, symmetry, artistic

Detail of the central platform of Ahu Tahira, showing the precise fitting of the stones

qualities, and attention to detail, this is undoubtedly the greatest architectural achievement of the island masons. Lamentably it survives today only as a ruin. A tradition collected by Mrs. Routledge relates that a group of Hanau Eepe lived at Vinapu for a time.[2] If they built this ahu it would seem that, though they were excellent craftsmen, they left something to be desired as sculptors. The statues on this most perfect of the ahu are not very well matched and are artistically inferior to many others on the island. In all, there are six, varying in height from about 10 to nearly 20 feet. There is space and a pedestal for another statue that appears never to have been erected. A seventh statue stands half buried in front of the ahu. Perhaps this was intended to complete the group.

The other especially remarkable example was Ahu Tongariki, which was situated near the bay at Hotu Iti at the eastern end of the south coast. The past tense is used advisedly, for this great structure was entirely destroyed by the tidal wave that struck the island on the night of May 22, 1960. This inundation resulted from a severe earthquake that caused great damage in continental Chile at the same time. Unfortunately Ahu Tongariki was located on a site just above sea level. Luckily no one was nearby at the time and the tragedy took place unseen, but a wall of water many feet high must have passed over the ahu leaving not one stone upon another. It is impossible to determine where the original foundations stood. Precisely cut and fitted stone blocks weighing many tons, and fifteen statues weighing some 60 tons each, were picked up like corncobs and tossed as far as a hundred yards inland. The great vesicular basalt blocks and the statues, which are among the most perfectly executed sculptures on the island, now lie scattered about as an awe-inspiring tribute to the power of the sea. This great ahu with its platform 475 feet long and more than 13 feet high was not as beautifully constructed as that at Vinapu, though there were many well-cut and well-fitted stones in it. If it was built by the Hanau Momoko, its remains suggest that they were better sculptors than architects.

Some of the ahu moai—I do not know how many—are so

oriented that their façades face the rising or setting sun at the equinox or the summer or winter solstices. What bearing this had on earlier beliefs is not known. Ahu Tahira at Vinapu is oriented toward the rising sun at the southern summer solstice, while another in the group faces the rising sun at the equinox.[3]

Three other kinds of ahu probably belong, not to the period of greatest architectural excellence, but to a later time when the island was devastated by internal conflicts and ambitious construction projects were impossible. These are the rectangular ahu, semi-pyramidal ahu, and *ahu poepoe*. Most are built of relatively small stone masonry and possess little architectural merit. The rectangular ahu are rubble-filled flat-topped platforms, usually 3 to 6 feet high, 10 to 13 feet wide, and sometimes as much as 100 feet in length. They served as burial places and contain one or more stone-lined tombs. Most are located near the coasts.

Mrs. Routledge coined the name "semi-pyramidal ahu" for a kind of small stone masonry structure that exists on the island in about forty-five examples.[4] These structures have the form of a low, extremely elongated half-pyramid. On the side which usually faces the sea they present a long slightly sloping wall highest in the center. The land side presents two sloping surfaces that meet each other in a wide angle. Most of the larger ones are about 120 to 150 feet long and 6 to 10 feet high; others are no more than 30 masonry feet in length. They usually contain one or more lined tombs. Occasionally these ahu have placed upon them fragments of broken statues, vertically placed stones, or, rarely, rows of small cairns. Some are built over ahu moai and thus suggest relatively recent construction.

Of considerably more artistic interest are the ahu poepoe, of which there are only seven on the island. These are also of rubble-filled small-stone masonry and are somewhat similar in form to the rectangular ahu, the difference being that one end is elevated—occasionally both ends are—and the flat upper surface is thus curved from end to end, recalling the shape of the square-ended boats, which in the old form of the language were also called poepoe. These ahu also have stone-lined tombs in them and are occasionally surmounted by fragments of old statues or vertically placed stones. One beautiful example a short distance west of Anakena is constructed on an elevated rock close to the coast, as if it were ready to launch itself on the waves of the sea to carry its deceased passengers to some far-away coast. It is 69 feet long, about 13 feet high, and the bow is elevated about 4 feet above the stern. These ahu again have always seemed to me another example of the sea-going orientation so evident in much of the thinking of the islanders.

Another type of structure, which perhaps should not be classified properly as an ahu, is called an *avanga*. These are relatively small rectangular or irregular structures, usually of small-stone masonry. Many are associated with ahu of other kinds, while others occur in isolation. Some are elevated on natural stone outcroppings. There appear to be two kinds of these. One typically contains a stone-lined tomb; the other has on top one or more rectangular or irregular cysts in which cremations appear to have been made. Some of these are similar to and may be related to the cremation cysts that I mentioned earlier as being located in front of many ahu moai.

The religious monuments of the island are in truth remarkable works of art and architecture, especially in view of the fact that they were made by such a tiny community, remote from outside stimuli, and in a land so poor in natural resources. Even more remarkable is the fact that they do not appear to have been the products of a public-works-minded island-wide authority. The ariki henua, as I have said, were not political rulers but sacred repositories of mana. Thus the monuments would seem to have been built independently by local kin-groups in the territories where they were located. This would suggest that the builders of any one structure were not the population of the island at large but rather a relatively small group of kinsmen. Perhaps there was cooperation among these groups, but we do not know to what extent. There are memories among the islanders of the former ownership of certain ahu by still surviving families.

But our admiration for these achievements is inevitably accompanied by a great sadness engendered by their lamentable state of destruction. The statues have been toppled from their pedestals and many lie broken on the ahu ramps. Stone topknots which once rested on the heads of statues sometimes have rolled many yards inland. Great fitted stones have been wrenched violently from their seats and remain scattered about in disarray, for the most part as a result of later local warfare. Thanks to the lively interest in the island and its monuments demonstrated by the Government of Chile, it seems likely that systematic conservation measures will be carried out soon, and many of the ahu will probably be restored completely. One day in the future the monuments may again be seen as they were during the time they were in use. Only then can the architectural accomplishments of the people who created them be properly understood.

NINE

The Great Statues

IN DISCUSSING THE RELIGIOUS AND MORTUARY ARCHITECTURE OF EASTER Island, I have mentioned the great statues only in passing. Since the time of Roggeveen, these statues have been almost the only thing the world has known about Easter Island. I suppose that for all time the classic symbol of Easter Island will be a gigantic brooding moai, his lips curled with disdain, gazing out to sea from the slopes of Rano Raraku. Perhaps this is rightly so, for the carving, transportation, and erection of these gigantic monuments were an accomplishment worthy of the highest admiration.

The statues are unique. There is nothing quite like them anywhere else, nor is there any locality to which one can point and say, "This is the source of the ideas from which they were developed." Large stone statues are found on the Marquesas, Raivavae, and perhaps other islands in eastern Polynesia. Never do they occur in sizes or numbers approaching those of Easter Island, and their form is considerably different from that of the moai. In many localities in western South America monolithic sculpture was common, but there too the styles are different, and no detailed similarities to the classic moai have been found.[1] The distinctive style of the Easter Island statues seems to be a local development.

Tradition states that the art of carving stone statues was known to the colonists who came with Hotu Matu'a, and, in fact, preserves the names of several statues, especially one called Tauto, which at the time of the immigration were left behind in Hiva. Hotu Matu'a is said to have sent back a special expedition to obtain these. Perhaps some day these statues will be found, and if so they may tell us something about the source of the artistic heritage that produced the moai. But truly large stone sculpture does not seem to have been made, at least to any significant extent, at the time of the colonization. The privileged title of *maori anga moai*, or master sculptor, did not yet exist. The style and the engineering of the great statues developed later.

The art of carving large statues flowered along with that of building the great ahu. Its purpose appears to have been to commemorate illustrious ancestors of the various kin-groups, whose mana was thought to bring benefit to the communities. Perhaps the statues also gratified the vanity of the owners of the ahu on which they were placed, thus stimulating them to produce larger and more perfect works of art than those of their neighbors. Whatever the cause, an obsessive enthusiasm appears to have taken possession of both Hanau Momoko and Hanau Eepe, resulting in a happy competition and cooperation between the sculptors and artisans of the two groups. Only in this manner can be explained the astounding fact that on an island so small, with a population that could never have exceeded 3000 or 4000, there were produced well over 600 statues now known and probably many more that remain to be discovered.

It is quite natural that the eighteenth-century European explorers who first saw the island received the impression that the statues were idols. The foreigner commonly expects this in a primitive and pagan community, and the idea was quite naturally reinforced by the sight of great numbers of gigantic moai. But in reality no moai is known to have borne the name of a divine personality, such as the creator god Makemake. All were known by the general name of *aringa ora*, which literally translated signifies "living faces." These were figures which served to maintain alive the memory of the

Heads of buried moai protruding from the flank of the Rano Raraku quarry

At Ahu Akivi the seven moai
were re-erected when the altar was
restored in 1960

(LEFT) *The flank of the Rano Raraku quarry;*
(BELOW) *part of the quarry and crater*

When work at the quarry suddenly ceased,
some moai were left unfinished

Other moai, ready to be transported to their destinations,
were never detached from their positions in the quarry

Abandoned topknots, intended for moai,
line the prehistoric road leading from
the quarry at Punapau where the topknots were carved

(LEFT) *Unique among Easter Island statues, this kneeling bearded man may represent one of the singers at special festivals called riu*
(BELOW) *A moai from Ahu Tongariki, which was thrown 100 yards inland by the tidal wave which destroyed the ahu in 1960*

*Recently restored, this moai with topknot in place
stands on Ahu ko te Riku at Tahai*

ancestors. The islanders may have of course possessed some sort of special religious cult devoted to ancestors; such cults are widely found in Polynesia. However, if one existed on Easter Island nothing is known of its practices. Behrens wrote in 1772 that when the ships of Roggeveen first dropped anchor, probably off the coast of Hotu Iti, he saw that the islanders built fires at the feet of their "idols" and that on the following day they did it again; "apparently," he says, "to offer morning sacrifices in honor of their Gods."[2] As Behrens had no information about what he saw, this is not sufficient proof of the existence of a cult of ancestors. Another explanation is possible. The unusual arrival of three great ships, such as no one on the island had seen before, must have filled the people with fear. They would have been concerned to assure the friendliness of such strangers. They may well have lit the fires to prepare earth ovens so that they could offer food. Behrens also mentions that the islanders brought aboard great quantities of tubers and many chickens cooked according to their manner.[3]

A few statues are made of stone of different kinds from a variety of locations. Most of these may well be some of the first statues made. Quite early in the development of the art, however, the islanders appear to have settled upon a single standard material, since the vast majority of the statues and all the very large ones are made of this. This material is the compact tuff from the cone of the great volcano Rano Raraku, on the eastern part of the south coast not far from the foot of Poike. On both the exterior and interior slopes of the southern side of the crater are the remains of extensive quarries. Everywhere are to be seen quarried faces where statues have been removed, and some 200 statues in various stages of completion remain in the quarries. A good many others will probably be found when excavations are made in the quarry debris. The largest of these unfinished statues is about 65 feet long and must weigh many hundreds of tons.

At the bottom of the crater slope about seventy statues remain standing. The largest is over 35 feet high. Many are deeply buried in the talus, and future investigations will probably reveal still others now completely buried. In the vicinity about thirty additional ones lie on the surface. These may have been ready to be transported to ahu.

As the quarry illustrates beautifully every stage of the carving process, the way in which the statues were made can be described with considerable accuracy. Most, though not all, were carved face up and in a horizontal or slightly sloping position. A channel large enough to accommodate the workmen was excavated around and under each statue in such a manner as to leave it attached to the living rock only by a narrow keel along its back. Practically all the carving of the figure, including fine detail, was completed at this stage. The statue was then detached from its keel and slid down the slope of the volcano. The carving and the excavation of the channel was done with adzes of basalt which are called *toki*. This hard, fine-grained material is found as nodules in the tuff and also in abundance in other parts of the island. In the vicinity of the quarry thousands of these tools are found just as they were discarded by the workmen who used them.

With one curious exception about which I shall speak later, the statues that were produced here are all of one highly developed style. In essential features they are very similar to one another. They are standing figures with bases at about the level of the hips. Arms hang stiffly at the sides and the extended hands with long and slender fingers are turned unnaturally toward each other across the lower part of the protruding abdomen. The heads are elongated and rectangular with heavy brows and prominent, usually slightly concave noses. The small, thin-lipped mouths are pursed to convey a disdainful expression. Chins are prominent. The ear lobes are elongated in the style I mentioned earlier as having been introduced by the Hanau Eepe, and some are carved to represent inserted ear ornaments. Hands, breasts, navels, and facial features are precisely indicated, and backs are sometimes beautifully carved to represent tattooed designs.

Within this stylistic framework there are many individual differences. No two statues are exactly alike. Some are slender and finely executed, revealing the touch of the true artist, while others appear less well conceived and more ordinary in aspect. Some are extraordinarily broad and corpulent. Perhaps these represent Hanau Eepe.

The one exception in the Rano Raraku quarry to this stylistic form is truly odd and of a unique style. It was discovered and excavated by Arne Skjölsvold, an archaeologist who came with Heyerdahl's expedition.[4] This statue reveals the full figure of a man kneeling, his buttocks resting on his heels and his hands extended along the sides of his thighs. The head is rounded and stylistically unlike those of the other statues, and the ears do not appear to be artificially elongated. The chin bears a small goatee. The total height is slightly over 14 feet.

The peculiar posture of this statue is well known on Easter Island and is called *tuku turi* or simply *tuku*. It was the posture used by the men and women who formed the chorus in the festivals called *riu*, where the posture was known as *tuku riu*. Typical also of the singers was the slight backward inclination of the trunk, the raised head, and the goatee, all also seen in the statue. Islanders of today remember having heard their elders tell that the singers were accustomed to wear masks, with beards made of a tuft of women's hair tied to the chin. It seems likely that this statue represents a riu singer and was made after the production of classic statues had ceased. Perhaps it commemorated something related to these singing festivals that were so important a diversion well into historic times.

About the means of transporting the statues and erecting them on ahu little is known. However it was done, it represents an engineering achievement that excites great admiration. Over 324 examples were either placed on ahu pedestals or are lying along prehistoric roads in various parts of the island. These latter were apparently abandoned in transportation. Many statues weighing scores of tons were transported to all parts of the island along prepared roads, some

The topknot quarry at Pinapau

of which can be seen today. The largest statue to have been transported to an ahu is the single specimen at Ahu Te Pito Kura on the north coast. This gigantic monolith, said to have been called Paro, has been calculated to weigh in the vicinity of 82 tons.[5] To have been brought from Rano Raraku it must have been moved nearly 4 miles. This is a really formidable feat of engineering.

There has been much speculation on methods of transportation. Judging by the many examples abandoned along roads, the statues appear to have been moved in a prone position and head first. An important part of the enigma involved the fact that the statues were moved after even the fine detail of their carving was complete. To move them without damaging their delicately prepared surfaces must have been no easy problem. Perhaps they were pulled by many men on some sort of sledge. The traditions relate that transportation was accomplished through the power of the mana of the priests, who were able to make the statues walk a short distance each day until eventually they reached the ahu.

The erection of the statues on the ahu also obviously presents serious engineering problems. Since the islanders had no cranes or similar heavy equipment, it seems most probable that the statues were elevated onto their ahu pedestals by levering them up in tiny stages and gradually building under them a platform of masonry which eventually would permit them to be tipped into place.

Perhaps the greatest engineering achievement of all was the placing on the heads of some statues on ahu large cylindrical topknots of red scoria. These sometimes had rabbeted tops and intricately carved surfaces. In the local language they were called *ha'u moai*. This may have been a custom developed fairly late in the statue-building period, for many of the statues on ahu apparently did not have them. Fifty-eight of these topknots apparently once rested on statues. About twenty-five remain in or near the quarry where they were carved. This quarry is located on the southern part of the west coast near a small natural well called Punapau. That name today is also commonly used for the quarry, which, like that at Rano

Raraku, is associated with a volcanic crater. The topknots were carved in much the same manner as the statues, by excavating a channel around them and breaking them loose. Being cylindrical they could be rolled relatively easily to their ahu locations. Here again we have only what tradition tells us to explain how they were placed on the heads of the statues. It is related that a causeway of dry masonry was erected to the head of the statue, long enough to provide a grade up which the topknots could be rolled. If this was the method used, it must have been difficult indeed, for some of the topknots are very large and heavy. The one worn by the statue Paro at Ahu Te Pito Kura is about 6 feet high and nearly 7 feet in diameter. It has been calculated to weigh over 11 tons.[6]

The work system used to carve the great statues and construct the ahu was probably that used today by the islanders when they require the cooperation of many people. For such tasks groups of kinsmen were brought together. The *tangata honui*, the leaders of the kin-groups, certainly had sufficient authority to bring together the necessary people. The workers were not paid with money, which happily did not exist in those days, but rather with an abundance of food, which was what represented value to these people. In order to maintain the morale of the crew bountiful preparation of the *umu tahu*, as this kind of earth oven and also the food cooked in it were called, was necessary to satisfy the hearty appetites of the crew both morning and evening. I should add also that the workers expected to obtain supernatural benefits for their efforts. They were not slaves laboring under the lash but people who felt that they were working for themselves and undoubtedly enjoyed what they were doing.

A significant aspect of all this artistic and architectural work is that it must have had an important relation to the economy of the island at large. For relatively small kin-groups to maintain crews of sculptors at Rano Raraku, people to transport statues, and artisans to build ahu must have required that a considerable proportion of the population devote its efforts to religious building activities. These

Moai in front of the Rano Raraku quarry

people had to be supported by others, and remarkably efficient soil cultivation and fishing operations had to be maintained. The tradition mentions *tangata heuheu henua* who devoted themselves to the cultivation of the land and *tangata tere vaka* who were specialists in fishing. After all, it was the effective production of these two groups that permitted others to create the fantastic quantity of art and architecture that remains today.

As seems always to be true of the golden age of every civilization, this one too came to a sudden end. Its grandeur and undoubtedly its pride were dashed to the ground by a series of misfortunes that eventually reduced to a tiny remnant these people at the center of the world.

The Great Statues   127

TEN

The Beginning of the End

THE SPECTACULAR ACHIEVEMENTS OF THE PEOPLE OF EASTER ISLAND APPEAR to have developed gradually, after a long period of learning how to live on the island. It was necessary first to develop effective methods of fishing and cultivation of the soil; then the population began to increase. A point was eventually reached when a numerous population had developed a cooperative way of life and an economy so effective that great numbers of people could devote their time, not to the production of food, but to the building of great architectural and artistic works. The golden age of most effective exploitation of the resources of the island had arrived, and life was good. Such a balance is always difficult to achieve and even more difficult to maintain. Here it was destroyed by a series of events that were devastating in their effect. Perhaps food supply may have had something to do with setting off the animosities that developed the troubles. The population must have reached its highest level at this time, and, in efforts to maintain the traditional religious building, competition for food resources may have produced dissension. Whatever the causes, the golden age appears to have come to a rather abrupt end.

Even casual visitors to the island gather this impression from the things they see around them. The hundreds of statues in every stage of completion in the quarry at Rano Raraku strongly suggest that the crews of workers might all have laid down their tools and departed on a single day. Along the roads of the island many statues appear to have been abandoned en route to ahu, some within a short distance of the pedestal where they were destined to stand. Some of the ahu remain in a state of partial completion, while others appear to have been violently destroyed, with their statues toppled and their masonry torn apart. Clearly something happened here which laid waste the early achievements.

The tradition as it was told to me gives some light but not nearly as much as we would like. It tells of a bloody battle between the Hanau Eepe and the Hanau Momoko, which resulted in the almost total extermination of the former. Something of the cause is recounted. The Hanau Eepe are said to have been an energetic and arrogant group with a tendency toward domination. They conceived the really excellent idea of gathering up and throwing into the sea the millions of stones that litter the surface of the island and make agriculture difficult. It is possible that they may actually have done this on the slopes of Poike, which in its lack of stones presents a sharp contrast to other parts of the island. They appear to have wanted the Hanau Momoko to aid in this work or to do it for them. The latter did not take kindly to the idea and answered, "No, we discovered this island. Our ariki, Hotu Matu'a, who was a Hanau Momoko, discovered it. We will not give this, our island, to you." This part of the tradition clearly shows the exasperation of the Hanau Momoko with the domineering attitude of the Hanau Eepe.

Another version of the tradition suggests other motives. The Hanau Eepe, who lived principally in the area of Poike, had mixed to some extent with other groups, and some individuals or families resided in other parts of the island. One of them, called Ko Ita, made his home in Orongo on the lip of the crater of Rano Kau. According to the story, it became known that he had secreted in his house the corpses of thirty Hanau Momoko children which he had killed in order to eat them. Among his victims were seven children of a Hanau Momoko man called Ko Pepe. The latter went berserk with sorrow when he learned what had been done and eventually died. His kinsmen in vengeance killed all the Hanau Eepe who lived on the Rano Kau slope between Orongo and Vinapu. As a result, all the other Hanau Eepe who were dispersed in various locations over the island took refuge with their kinsmen on the slopes of Poike.

Though, like much legendary information, this account may be distorted, it probably casts some light on the forms of expression of animosities which may have been motivated by deeper problems. The population must have been large at this time, and competition for farm lands and fishing rights was probably becoming intense. The balance between population and resources was undoubtedly approaching a critical point.

The practice of cannibalism may have been brought to the island by the Hanau Eepe. Tradition affirms that it did not exist in the time of Hotu Matu'a, though, at least by the time of the troubles, it had certainly been adopted by various families among the Hanau Momoko.

For whatever reasons, the Hanau Eepe found themselves in a state of siege on Poike. The promontory was probably as good a place to defend as the island afforded. It includes the smooth slopes of the great volcano that forms the eastern corner of the island. Here the terrain rises in a smooth gradual ascent to the lip of the volcano over 1300 feet above sea level. The shores consist of high and rugged cliffs difficult of ascent and possessing no good landing places for watercraft. The point most vulnerable to attack is the foot of the western or inland slope of the volcano. Even here the terrain is unbroken, and any group movement of the enemy could easily be seen from higher elevations. Expecting an attack by the much more numerous Hanau Momoko, the Hanau Eepe, according to tradition, excavated across the foot of this slope a series of trenches extending all the way across the island from Mahatua to Te Hakarava. The spoil was thrown on the uphill side, and the enemy would have faced first a trench and then a steep slope formed of the spoil pile, behind which the defenders could have concealed themselves. Twenty-six of these trenches, separated by short unexcavated intervals, may be distinguished today in this location. They appear originally to have been about 16 feet wide and 10 or 12 feet deep. They are now almost completely filled by natural deposits.

The line, over 2 miles long, would have required a great many men to defend it and would presumably have dispersed any defending force prohibitively. Some observers have suggested that the excavations may have been made originally at an earlier time to capture moisture for the cultivation of bananas or other crops and were later used by the Hanau Eepe for defense.

The tradition relates that the Hanau Eepe placed in these trenches a great quantity of wood and other vegetation which they proposed to ignite in case of an attack by the Hanau Momoko. But when the Hanau Momoko did attack, a trick of war and the astuteness of a woman caused the tables to be turned and the Hanau Eepe to be burned in their own fire. To this day the trenches are called *Te Umu o te Hanau Eepe*, which means "the earth oven of the Hanau Eepe."

The story runs as follows: "A Hanau Eepe man who lived on the slopes of Poike had with him on the Poike slope a Hanau Momoko woman who worked for him as a cook. On the upper side of the trenches were the Hanau Eepe while on the lower side were the Hanau Momoko. This woman, called Moko Pinge'i felt very sorry for her people, who were the Hanau Momoko.

"In the night she passed secretly by way of the coast and arrived among the Hanau Momoko. She greeted them and cried with sorrow. The Hanau Momoko said to Moko Pinge'i, 'How can we surprise the Hanau Eepe?' Moko Pinge'i answered, 'Watch me, and when you see me sitting and weaving a basket that will be the signal that they are all sleeping. Send your men then to the attack.' The Hanau Momoko said, 'We agree.' Moko Pinge'i returned to the house of the man of the Hanau Eepe for whom she worked and remained there waiting. On the following day, very early in the morning, the Hanau Momoko saw that Moko Pinge'i was seated and was weaving a basket. They attacked by way of both coasts, passing through Te Hakarava and Mahatua in a pincers movement. Some remained in front of the trenches to show themselves to the Hanau Eepe. The latter came to fight the Hanau Momoko that they saw before them in front of the fire. Those Hanau Momoko who had come by way of Te Hakarava and Mahatua attacked from behind and from both sides. The Hanau Eepe did not see them because they were fighting against those in front. When the Hanau Eepe tried to retreat toward the sides, they became aware that the way was closed by the enemy. They turned to fight against those Hanau Momoko who were advancing from behind, but these gave no ground. They were not afraid but enclosed the Hanau Eepe by advancing from Te Hakarava and Mahatua and coming together in the center. They threw the Hanau Eepe into the trenches. As if they were stones they threw them down into the fires. The Hanau Eepe were finished. They died. The trenches were filled and the good odor of the cooked meat of the Hanau Eepe rose into the air.''

The tradition goes on to relate that three of the Hanau Eepe men escaped death in the fires in the trenches. They fled and concealed themselves in a cave. Two of them were killed by their pursuers. Only one man, called Ororoina, survived. The Hanau Momoko were moved by his desperate cries and they let him live, saying, "We will leave him unharmed and he may have descendants." Ororoina went to live in the house of a certain Pipi Horeko, who lived at Maunga Toatoa near Rano Raraku. He married a woman of the Hanau Momoko of the family of a man called Haoa and had many descendants.

It is related that in later years some of the Hanau Momoko decided that Ororoina had had too many descendants, and in order to decrease the numbers of this issue of their enemies they placed thirty of them in a house and set fire to the thatch. All but one were suffocated. A certain Ure o Pea, who may have been a grandson of Ororoina, managed to escape. His son bore the name Ko Pea ko te Motuha o te Koro, which means "Pea who distributes food at the koro festival." He gave this festival to the people of his family in memory of the escape of his father. As sponsor of the koro he distributed food among the guests. His son was Inaki Uhi, and one of Inaki Uhi's sons was Ao Ngatu. One of the sons of Ao Ngatu, who was called Hare Kai Hiva, was born near the beginning of the nineteenth century. He received Christian baptism and was given the name Atamu, or Adam. He was the great-grandfather and great-great-grandfather of a family numerous on the island today and now called Atan.

The genealogy of this family makes it possible to calculate approximately the date of the battle at Poike. Allowing twenty-five to thirty years for each generation, Ororoina would have been born in the latter half of the seventeenth century. This calculation has been confirmed by excavations in the Poike trenches carried out in 1955 by Carlyle Smith, an archaeologist with Heyerdahl's expedition. He obtained a charcoal sample in one of the trenches from what appeared to have been the remains of a large conflagration, and it revealed a radiocarbon date of 1676 A.D., plus or minus 100 years.[1]

Thus it would seem that only a short time after this battle the island saw the first of the four eighteenth-century visits which I mentioned in Chapter 1.

The conclusion of the tradition of the fate of the Hanau Eepe includes an interesting minor detail, which, oddly enough, is supported from another source. It is related that a descendant of Ororoina was the first man to go aboard the first of the strange ships. The words of the tradition as I heard it are: "They gave him liquid and food but he did not eat or drink. He took the liquid and washed himself with it by pouring it over his head." This same incident is described in Behrens' account of the arrival of the ships of Roggeveen in 1722. "Next day we stood in with our ships to look for a harbour, whereupon one of the natives came off in a small skiff [schiffgen] to meet us some two miles off the land. We took him aboard our vessel and gave him a piece of linen cloth to wrap about his body, for he was quite naked, and we offered him beads and other trinkets, all of which he hung around his neck together with a dried fish. He was very regularly and cleverly painted with all sorts of figures: he was of a brown tint, and had long ears which hung down as far as his shoulders as if they had been stretched to that length by being weighted, after the fashion of the Mongolian Moors. He was fairly tall in stature, strong in limb, of good appearance, and lively in mien, as well as pleasing in speech and gesture. We gave this South Lander or foreign visitor a glass of wine to drink; but he only took it and tossed it into his eyes, whereat we were surprised. I fancy he thought that we designed to poison him by this means, which is a common usage among Indians."[2]

The preservation in island memory of this isolated incident is not surprising. Roggeveen's visit was the most extraordinary of events, and it can readily be imagined that many people surrounded the descendant of Ororoina upon his return to the land to hear what he had to tell of those strange people. Naturally he related everything, and in this small world no detail was lost. There was not a house or a cave on the island in which his story was not commented upon over and over again.

Whether the battle at Poike was the first one, or only one of a series of conflicts preparing the way for the disintegration of the island's culture is not known. It is the one which tradition has preserved, and there were more misfortunes to follow.

ELEVEN

Conflict and Cannibalism

IN THE BLOODY BATTLE AT THE FOOT OF POIKE, THE HANAU MOMOKO HAD AN opportunity to satiate their feelings of hatred and vengeance toward the Hanau Eepe and to rejoice in being victors and undisputed owners of the island. Perhaps tranquillity and peace returned for a time, but not for long. As violence seems to breed more violence, there appears to have been little delay in fomenting discord, rivalry, and animosity among the Hanau Momoko themselves. The various kin-groups appear to have turned on one another, and the picture begins to be one of more or less continuous strife, in which no man was safe away from his kinsmen, and the continuation of construction of great public works became impossible. Under the conditions that prevailed, unprotected crews could not be sent to carve statues at Rano Raraku; access to the roads used for transporting statues was not safe.

The most characteristic theme of the traditions of this period, as I have heard them, is that of the ascendancy to power of the *matatoa*. These were the strongest of the island's warriors and were essentially professional fighters, who probably did no other work. Their presence in a battle was considered to ensure victory. In these troubled times the fear they inspired and the prestige they gained enabled them to acquire ever greater control over the ariki and the priesthoods, who formerly provided through their mana the sources of social control. People gathered around these warriors and sought their protection from the depredations of other groups. They were called *tangata rima toto*, "men with bloody hands," because of their violent dispositions and deeds of vengeance and cruelty. Some of these matatoa appear to have become the actual rulers of the kin-groups in the fluid conditions of the times. There is no direct legendary evidence that any matatoa was ever undisputed ruler over the whole island, but there are indirect suggestions that some may have approached this at least temporarily. The various communities scattered over the island became more and more like predatory bands, and much of the older, more ordered way of life gradually vanished. Encroachment on the land or fishing areas of others became even more strongly resented, and retaliation was swift and violent. The land areas and fishing zones to which the different groups were permitted access were precisely marked. Conflicts arose for the most unimportant reasons. Fancied insults and rumors of plans for depredations were taken up instantly as provocation for retaliation. Flaming desire for revenge served to keep emotions at high intensity. Though ritual cannibalism may have been present earlier, this practice now increased greatly, and the emphasis changed to more secular food cannibalism.

All this suggests that the island was suffering from overpopulation. Probably during the period of great public works a nicely balanced organization provided food for everyone. This became harder to maintain as numbers increased. When violence disrupted the balance, much food-producing work became more difficult or impossible, with crops being burned or otherwise destroyed, and quite suddenly all the people suffered sharply increased deprivation. Attempts to alleviate this by more violence against neighbors further disrupted food production, and the situation became progressively worse.

The example set by the first visits of the Europeans may also have contributed to the development of this atmosphere of violence.

Beginning with the arrival of Roggeveen, the islanders were subjected to inhuman acts that had no reason or justification. Behrens relates that, before Roggeveen's party had even landed, one of the islanders who came to observe the strange ship was shot with a musket. Behrens did not know why. On the following day, when the commander came on shore with about 150 of his men, the islanders immediately gathered in a great crowd on the beach. This was certainly to have been expected, for everyone must have wanted to see these strange people and the unfamiliar things they wore and carried. Some islanders tried in their curiosity to touch the weapons of the visitors. They were fired upon, and many were wounded and some killed.[1] This very first encounter presented the islanders with clear evidence that men from other lands did not respect the lives of those around them. During the next 150 years they were to receive many more object lessons of this kind.

The weapons used by the islanders in their own conflicts were primitive but deadly. Both traditions and archaeological evidence suggest that some of them at least may have been newly developed at the time of the internal conflicts to meet the problems that arose. One such weapon was the *mataa,* a large crudely percussion-flaked spearhead with a projecting tang made of the abundantly available obsidian. Though most of these have been picked up and carried away by recent visitors, they used to be scattered over the surface of the island in endless numbers. Tremendous quantities of them must have been made. Though obsidian tools of many kinds are found buried in the earlier archaeological deposits, the mataa do not appear there. They seem to have come into use shortly before the arrival of the first Europeans. They were attached to short handles to make the so-called *kakau* for hand-to-hand combat or to longer shafts to make deadly throwing spears called *mataa ko hou.* These large blades are described as producing ghastly wounds with their ragged, razor-sharp edges. Also in use were wooden clubs called *paoa.* These were short, flat weapons with tapered edges, similar in form to a rather blunt sword or cutlass. Blows were struck with the edges and could easily fracture a skull or break an arm or leg. Those who carried this weapon were called *tangata paoa*, or simply *paoa*, a term which seems to have been applied in a general sense of warriors who ranked below the matatoa.

To protect themselves from aggression the kin-groups depended on the bravery and skill of their sons, and these were systematically trained. They were brought together frequently for practice in the arts of war. There were specially designated instructors called *mata'u*, who first taught the youths to throw and to dodge shafts which had gourds attached to their heads. Later shafts with small mataa attached were used, and finally the standard weapon. This training is said to have developed in the young men an almost incredible skill in the art of dodging thrown spears. The fathers of the youths were present at these exercises and were proud when their sons distinguished themselves by their proficiency in attack or defense. When young men were wounded in training or conflict they were attended by specialists in the curing of wounds, who were called *tangata rara haoa*. Such war games were favorite amusements at feasts, not only for the young, but also for mature men.

Before going out to fight, the youths were required to pass a night of vigil—a rather more complicated one than that of Don Quixote in the courtyard of the inn. On this night each father prepared for his son a white rooster cooked in an earth oven, and the young man ate some of the meat. White chickens were thought of as lucky and as providing protection in combat. When the young warriors went out to the fight they were accompanied by both male and female sorcerers, who remained on a nearby hill and recited charms to bring victory. The women and children also watched the conflicts from convenient vantage points.

During these times there appear to have been many battles between kin-groups, which were local and mostly of short duration. There was undoubtedly at least one actual war that lasted a considerable time and had devastating effects. This was fought between groups of the northwest coast and others of the southeast. The prin-

A late-eighteenth-century Easter Islander with elongated earlobes (from James Cook, Second Voyage . . . Round the World . . ., 1777)

cipal antagonists, called Poie and Kainga, are well remembered. We can deduce with some accuracy that this war must have occurred between 1771 and 1773, because none of the members of the Gonzalez expedition, which came to the island in 1770, mentions any evidence of conflict or its effects, at least during the few hours they were ashore. However, Captain Cook, who arrived four years later, conveys in his whole account the strong impression that the island had just suffered a serious major conflict.[2] This deduction coincides with the traditional information that this war was in the time of the ariki Tu'u ko Iho. This was not the famous first sculptor of the moai kavakava who accompanied Hotu Matu'a and whom I mentioned earlier, but another ariki of the same name who lived in the second half of the eighteenth century. A remembered genealogy relates that he was the great-great-grandfather of a certain Lázaro Neru who was born in 1860 and whose daughter Marina Neru was born in 1896 and is still living. During this war between the people of Poie and Kainga, it is said, cannibalism was first practiced on a grand scale. Though this cannibalism undoubtedly had its ritual aspects and served as an insult to the vanquished, many of the traditions suggest that human meat was highly prized as a delicacy among these people who had available so little mammalian flesh. It seems

Conflict and Cannibalism 141

likely that the development of the custom was related, at least in part, to food shortage.

Traditions relate that it was during this period of conflict that the ahu were destroyed and their statues toppled. This seems to have been a typical depredation of these intergroup conflicts. Perhaps the destruction of the statues of an enemy group was believed to obliterate the supernatural power of its ancestors and weaken its ability to resist. On the other hand, the cause may have been only an unfocused desire to destroy the valued property of an enemy. Whatever the reasons, during these conflicts excavations were made under statue pedestals and the statues made to fall, usually across the ahu ramps. Sometimes stones were deliberately positioned where statues were expected to fall, in order to break the statue across the neck and make re-erection impossible. Beautifully fitted basalt blocks of the ahu platforms were torn violently apart and left lying about. The thatched houses of the priests to landward of the ahu plazas were burned, and their carved foundation stones were sometimes carried away. Marks of these fires can be seen to this day on the precisely cut and fitted stones. This kind of depredation was the major cause of the present ruinous state of the monuments, though more recent vandalism by the islanders and others has contributed considerably.

Not all of this destruction appears to have been carried out at the same time. Some may have begun as early as the battle at Poike. Roggeveen did not mention having seen any fallen statues at Hotu Iti, but he was ashore only a few hours and saw only a tiny part of the island. Nor were any mentioned by the Gonzalez expedition. Officers of Captain Cook noticed three ahu on the south coast; on two of these all the statues were overthrown and on the third, one statue lay fallen. In other places they saw statues that were still in place on ahu.[3] In 1816 a Russian group saw two standing statues on the south coast.[4] In 1838 a Frenchman, Aubert du Petit-Thouars, saw statues still standing on the west coast.[5] Since then, no visitor has mentioned an intact ahu or a moai in place.

In 1915 an old islander told Mrs. Routledge that the last statue to be thrown down was the 82-ton Paro at Ahu Te Pito Kura which I mentioned earlier. The age of the islander at that time suggested that this must have happened around 1840. The statue was thrown down on the occasion of a conflict between west-coast and southeast-coast groups. The story told to Mrs. Routledge was that a woman of the west coast was killed and eaten by men of the southeast coast. Her son succeeded in trapping thirty of the enemy in a cave, and these were eaten in vengeance. It was in the conflict that ensued that the moai was thrown to the ground and broken across the neck.[6]

Though the statues on the slopes of Rano Raraku remained standing, all those on ahu were eventually toppled. Today the only statues standing on ahu are those which have been restored in modern times. In 1955 Pedro Atan, who was then mayor of the island, at the request of Thor Heyerdahl re-erected a single statue of about 25 tons weight on its pedestal on Ahu Ature Huki at Anakena. He did this in eighteen days with eleven assistants by levering it up in tiny stages and building a platform of stones under it.[7] His method was probably similar to that used in the original erection of the statues in prehistoric times. In 1960 Ahu Akivi, located inland of the central part of the west coast, was completely restored and its seven approximately 16-ton statues were re-erected by much the same methods.[8] Perhaps future restoration work will one day result in the rebuilding of the multitudes of ahu that line the coasts and the re-erection of the statues as they were before war took its toll. This would be a truly spectacular sight.

Thus, after a long period of working, building, learning, and striving to produce a way of life which provided well what they thought they needed and made possible public works that inspire the admiration even of those who see only their ruins, within a span of less than 200 years this once proud people was brought to the edge of extinction. Other factors contributed to this decline, among which we must count the activities of Europeans and their New World relatives.

ᴖ TWELVE

Final Tragedy

IN THE PRECEDING CHAPTER I DESCRIBED THE PERIOD OF DISORDER THAT developed after the great battle between the Hanau Eepe and the Hanau Momoko. This was a real time of cultural degeneration, and a strong tendency toward anarchy prevailed. The traditions relate that this reached such an extreme that in one of the wars of the early nineteenth century even the sacred person of Ngaara, the best-known of the later ariki henua, whose reign of several decades ended shortly before the arrival of the first missionary, was desecrated. He was abducted and carried from his sacred residence at Anakena into captivity in another part of the island. This event is sharply symptomatic of the extent to which the older values had become eroded. Remember that, though the ariki henua did not exercise political power and were not in any direct sense governors of the island's kin-groups, in earlier times their persons were the objects of profound respect. Formerly these personages had been tapu—sacred and untouchable.

Whether this change in the temper of the people had been brought about by overpopulation and competition for food resources or by some other cause, it carried with it the rise to power of numerous matatoa or war leaders, who controlled the various kin-groups. Their power appears to have developed a curious kind of ceremonial

145

reinforcement related to a religious cult that may have been present on the island for a considerable time previous to the rise of the matatoa. During the time of the troubles, at least, one matatoa was selected each year to hold a special office. By extension his kinsmen and friends wielded a power to carry out depredations which, though not very well understood today, appears to have been amplified greatly. The selected individual was called the *tangata manu*, or "bird man," and achieved this position each year in ceremonies dedicated to the cult of the *manutara* (sooty tern).

When this cult began and how it originated are not definitely known, but there is no doubt that in earlier times, before cultural disorganizations began, it had a different emphasis and a profoundly religious character. According to one tradition, the god Makemake brought from Motu Motiro Hiva (the old name of Sala y Gómez) the sooty terns which have since come to nest on Motu Nui and other islets. Even today their eggs are prized as a tasty addition to the meals of spring and summer.

The annual ceremonies of the cult were carried out at the unique village of Orongo, which apparently was used for no other purpose. In construction it is unlike anything else on the island. It lies on the narrow lip of the western side of the crater of Rano Kau. To the east a steep slope descends more than 650 feet to the surface of the volcano's crater lake, which is more than a half mile wide and is covered with a beautiful varicolored mat of totora reeds. To the west an almost vertical cliff descends more than 800 feet to the sea. The village site provides a breathtaking view of the three islets called Motu Nui, Motu Iti, and Motu Kaokao.

Here, scattered along the crest for over 800 feet, are about forty-seven houses and an ahu. The houses are long narrow ellipses somewhat similar in ground plan to the thatched dwellings scattered over the island, which I described earlier. Their construction, however, is quite different. The vertical walls are made of horizontally laid thin stone slabs, and the domed roofs are constructed of larger thin slabs interlocked and cantilevered to join at the center. Most are built so that one side is below ground while the other has a low entrance through which the visitor must crawl. Some of the houses have painted stone slabs inside.

A group of basalt outcroppings at the southern end of the village is decorated with a large number of petroglyphs in bas-relief depicting the tangata manu and other motifs. I shall discuss these later. At the northern edge is a small ahu overlooking the crater lake. It is associated with a kind of sundial which marks the position of the rising sun at the equinoxes and the summer and winter solstices.

In the month of September of each year, perhaps at the spring equinox, a ceremony was celebrated which began at Mataveri located at the foot of the northern slope of Rano Kau near the western shore of the island. Here the rituals were initiated with songs, feasting, and other activities. The participants later moved to Orongo to continue the rites.

For the ceremony the most important people of the various kin-groups were gathered together. These were the matatoa, who were accompanied by priests called *tumu ivi atua* and by some of the maori rongorongo, the custodians of the sacred inscribed tablets. At Orongo they occupied themselves with songs in honor of the god Makemake and with other related activities. Meanwhile certain servants of the matatoa, called *hopu manu* (servants of the bird), descended the cliff and swam to Motu Nui, where they waited for the first egg to be laid by a sooty tern. He who had the luck to find this first egg secured it and swam with it through the heavy seas and pounding breakers to the foot of the cliff and then scaled this difficult precipice in a climb few of us would care to make. When he reached Orongo he presented the egg to his matatoa who thereupon became the next tangata manu.

Some students of the ceremonies have suggested that the winning matatoa was regarded as the incarnation of the god Makemake. This would seem very probable, for from the moment of receiving the egg he became tapu and was henceforth regarded as sacred. Immediately there began a ceremonial procession amid the songs,

*Wooden effigy of a bird man;
about one-third actual size
(Peabody Museum, Harvard University*

cries, and gesticulations of the deliriously excited crowd. The bird man was escorted across the island to the stone quarry at Rano Raraku, where he lived during the following year in a special house in strict isolation. The stone foundation of this house is still standing.

The ceremony and the selection of the tangata manu must originally have been purely religious in character. This is certainly the impression one receives from the beautifully executed petroglyphs near the southern end of Orongo. Here are many bas-relief figures. The tradition relates that one was carved each year in commemoration of the newly selected tangata manu. They are human figures with bird heads or wearing bird masks, and each holds an egg in his elevated hands. They convey a feeling of reverence close to profound adoration.

These ceremonies and the feeling associated with them must have degenerated greatly during the period of internal troubles. In these later times the bird man not only had a sacred character but also the right, so called, to "hold the *ao*." An ao today is a heavy wooden club more than 3 feet in length with opposed faces carved on its handle. It is said formerly to have been an insignia of rank. The holding of the ao apparently meant that the tangata manu had power over the kin-groups of the island. As he had to remain in strict isolation, the power was actually wielded by his kin-group and others friendly to it. They exercised it in a brutal and ruthless way. Members of other kin-groups, and especially the important people in these, had to conceal themselves in caves to avoid becoming their victims. These defeated people were called *kio*. The marauders fell upon the members of other kin-groups like birds of prey. The cruelties committed by those of the groups that held the ao during the last decades of this period before the arrival of the missionaries were true atrocities. Father Hyppolyte Roussel wrote that the houses of the vanquished were burned and the people were carried away as slaves to work for their new masters. They were kept in caves from which they were released to work at cultivating crops. When their services were no longer needed they were occasionally set free; more often, however, they were subjected to horrifying treatment. The least of the acts of vengeance practiced against these unfortunate men, women, and children were blows with a club. Some were slashed and lacerated with obsidian blades. Others were burned over slow fires or trampled until their intestines were ground into the dirt. "All the cruel devices pagan barbarism could invent," said the missionary father, "were put to work against defenseless victims of all ages, sex and status."[1]

It is easy to understand why many islanders, especially women and mothers of families, felt and expressed their real happiness when, with the arrival of the missionaries and the introduction of Christianity, these acts of cruelty ceased.

As I suggested earlier, these acts of brutality may well have been encouraged by the examples set by the behavior of those who came on foreign ships during the early nineteenth century. Whalers and other vessels appeared from time to time, and some of the people who arrived on them behaved abominably. The traditions relate some of these events in considerable detail.

In the year 1805 the North American schooner *Nancy*, out of New London, Connecticut, came to the island with the object of enslaving some men and women to make them work in a sea-lion hunting project which they had planned on the island of Más Afuera in the Juan Fernández group. Sea-lion skins brought a good price in the market of that day. When these intruders arrived on shore near the present village of Hangaroa, the tradition describes a bloody battle with the islanders who had only their obsidian-tipped arms. Twelve men and ten women fell alive into the hands of these ruthless scoundrels. They were tied and carried aboard the *Nancy*, and not until after three days of sailing were their bonds removed. The men immediately took advantage of their liberty by diving overboard. The women were forcibly restrained from following them. The captain lowered a boat and pursued the fugitives, but whenever the boat approached a swimmer he dived under the water and evaded capture.[2]

Until recently all I knew of the fate of these unhappy men led me to believe that none had been able to save himself. Even if the schooner traveled slowly for lack of favorable winds, it seemed unlikely that the captain would have released his victims until he was sure that not even a Polynesian, to whom the sea was home, would think of trying to return by swimming. Not long ago I learned for the first time through two different accounts that the impossible, or that which would seem impossible, actually happened. One of these men survived and succeeded in returning to the island. In a family which today bears the name of Pate but which two or three generations ago was called Vaka Tuku Onge, it is remembered that three of their members were among these victims. One was more prudent than his companions. While the others began to swim as rapidly as they were able as soon as they were in the water, he moved slowly in order to conserve his strength. In vain he advised his friends to do the same, but one by one they disappeared beneath the waves. The account has preserved the details that the water was cold and that the few times he was able to urinate he captured the warm liquid and rubbed it on his stiffening limbs in an attempt to restore circulation. His fortitude was rewarded and he reached his home. This information from a tradition that appears to have been specially remembered by members of one family was independently confirmed in considerable detail by several other people still living today, who had heard the story from an old woman named Eva a Hey who died in 1946 at an age of at least 100 years.

About 1822 an unknown whaling vessel arrived at the island, and several young girls were carried aboard by force. The following day they were thrown into the water, and they also had to swim to shore.[3] One of the sailors of this same ship diverted himself by killing an islander with a rifle shot.

The most unhappy and most sharply remembered of all such events occurred between 1859 and 1862. During this period Peruvian ships came repeatedly to capture and carry away slaves needed to work at digging guano for fertilizer on the Chincha Islands near the coast of Peru. This developed into abduction on a grand scale. The arrival in December of 1862 of eight Peruvian slave ships at the same time is clearly remembered. When Mrs. Routledge was on Easter Island in 1914 there were several old people still alive who had seen with their own eyes the tragic events that took place, and these can be reconstructed from their stories. The slavers spread flashy and unfamiliar goods on the ground near the shore to entice incautious islanders from concealment. When a crowd of people had gathered, they were seized and tied and carried aboard ship. Those who resisted were shot. It is calculated that between 900 and 1000 islanders were carried into slavery at this time. The great majority of them died on the Chincha Islands of overwork, disease, and homesickness. Bishop Tepano Jaussen of Tahiti learned of this crime, and through his efforts France lodged a protest with the government of Peru. Shortly thereafter about 100 survivors were returned to the island, but the rescue was a little late. Most of them died during the return voyage, and only fifteen reached the island alive. They brought back with them smallpox and other diseases. Within a few years the epidemic that followed reduced the population of the island to a few hundred.[4]

The people taken as slaves to the Chincha Islands included not only the ariki henua Kai Makoi and his son Maurata, as I have mentioned, but also all the maori ko hau rongorongo, the masters of the art of writing. Thus the only real key to the decipherment of the sacred tablets disappeared only a very short time before the arrival of the missionaries who would have recorded it. Without doubt, a great many other individuals possessed of esoteric knowledge of one kind or another that would have gone far to solve the enigma of Easter Island also died either on the Chincha Islands or in the epidemic that followed the abduction. These events go far toward explaining why so much of the past of this island remains enveloped in mystery.

With these sad events the old culture came to an end. Thanks to the providence of God, shortly thereafter there arrived on the beach at Hangaroa the first missionary, Brother Eugène Eyraud, who with heroic patience dedicated himself to the instruction and well-being of the pagan islanders and thereby initiated the modern and Christian era.

In concluding this account of past times on Easter Island I want to emphasize strongly one final point. My interpretation of past events has been developed from what the islanders have told me and what I have read of the works of others, reinforced by my personal observations, impressions, and opinions. It does not represent any ultimate truth. It is what I have been able to learn and, as I have said, when the subject is enigmatic Easter Island no man's knowledge is complete or secure. Without doubt much that I have written will be modified as future investigation casts sharper light. I should like to remind you of the celebrated phrase of the Greek philosopher Heraclitus, *"panta rhei,"* which means literally that all things move and expresses the notion of continuous development in all things of the world, including the knowledge of men. Such development of knowledge, it has been said with considerable reason, consists of the constant correction of errors. With such corrections hopefully the future will make less opaque the veil of mystery through which we now see the past of Te Pito o Te Henua.

*Ruins of a stone-slab house at Orongo,
the village where the annual manutara ceremonies took place;
at left is the crater lake Rano Kau*

Petroglyphs at Orongo: (ABOVE) *a bird man;*
(RIGHT) *squatting bird men. The crater*
lake in the background is Rano Kau

West of Orongo lie the islets
Motu Nui, Motu Iti,
and Motu Kaokao.
On the largest,
Motu Nui,
the eggs of
the sooty tern
(manutara)
were sought
for the ceremonies
and brought back
to Orongo
by swimmers

Cave painting of sooty terns in Ana Kai Tangata; the name means
"cave where men are eaten"

In the district of Vaihu on the south coast of Easter Island,
moai toppled from an ahu still lie where they fell

Appendixes
Reference Notes
Glossary
Bibliography
Index

APPENDIX I. PEOPLE MENTIONED IN THE TEXT

This list includes traditional and historical names as well as those of recent or contemporary Easter Islanders. Since the early names are units, they are listed alphabetically under the first word of the name. Some of the later names consist of old family names combined with modern Christian names, but for consistency all are listed alphabetically by first name. Names of gods and other supernatural beings are not included in this appendix; these appear in the Glossary.

Ao Ngatu.   One of the descendants of *Ororoina*. He appears to have lived around the beginning of the nineteenth century. His father was *Inaki Uhi*.

Arturo Teao.   One of Father Sebastian's principal informants on traditions. He lived in the leprosarium and died some years ago.

Atamu.   See *Hare Kai Hiva*.

Ava Rei Pua.   A sister of *Hotu Matu'a*. She is mentioned in the tradition of his arrival as having immigrated to Easter Island with him.

Eva a Hey.   A descendant of a family of which several members were abducted by the schooner *Nancy* out of New London, Connecticut, in 1805. She died in 1946 at the age of at least 100 years.

Haoa.   Traditionally, the man to whose family *Ororoina's* wife belonged.

Hare Kai Hiva.   A descendant of *Ororoina*. Son of *Ao Ngatu*, he was baptized a Christian and was the first to bear the name *Atamu* (Adam). Atamu was later shortened to Atan and is a present-day family name.

Hau Maka.   According to tradition, a man living in Hiva who saw Easter Island in a dream and sent seven young men to make a reconnaissance of the island before the party of *Hotu Matu'a* departed.

Hotu Iti te Mata Iti.   Traditionally, the youngest son of *Hotu Matu'a.* At the time of the death of the latter he was given the district of Hotu Iti as his domain.

Hotu Matu'a.   Traditionally, the first ariki henua of Easter Island. He led a party from Hiva to the island.

Ika Uri.   A man who traditionally stole the hat of a foreign visitor at a place which still bears the name Ko te hikonga ha'u o Miti Rangi a Ika Uri.

Inaki Uhi.   Traditionally, a descendant of *Ororoina.* He was the son of *Ko Pea ko te Motuha o te Koro* and the father of *Ao Ngatu.*

Ira.   Traditionally, one of the young men sent by *Hau Maka* to make a reconnaissance of Easter Island.

Juan Araki.   An islander who died in 1949. He was shown a rongorongo tablet by *Paoa Hitaki.*

José Pate.   An islander who found a partly burned rongorongo tablet in the the ruins of a burned house near Hanga Hoonu in 1937.

Kai Makoi.   One of the last ariki henua. In 1862 he was enslaved by Peruvians and taken to the Chincha Islands where he died.

Kainga.   The leader of one of the opposing groups in a war that appears to have taken place between 1771 and 1773.

Ko Ita.   Traditionally, a Hanau Eepe man who made his home in Orongo and killed and ate Hanau Momoko children. This is said to have contributed to the animosities that culminated in the battle of Poike.

Ko Pea ko te Motuha o te Koro.   "Pea who distributes food at the koro festival." Traditionally the name of a descendant of *Ororoina. Inaki Uhi* was his son.

Ko Pepe.   Traditionally, a Hanau Momoko man whose children were eaten by *Ko Ita.*

Ku'uku'u.   Traditionally, one of the young men sent by *Hau Maka* to make a reconnaissance of Easter Island. He was wounded by a supernatural turtle and died before the arrival of *Hotu Matu'a.* He is remembered for having planted a yam patch on the slopes of Rano Kau.

Lázaro Neru.   An islander born in 1860, who is said to have been the great-great-grandson of an ariki named *Tu'u ko Iho* who lived in the eighteenth century (not the mau who accompanied *Hotu Matu'a*).

Maeha.   Traditionally, a man living in Hiva, from whom the yams brought to Easter Island by *Hotu Matu'a's* party were stolen.

Maramara Kai.   Traditionally, the wife of *Nuku Kehu.* She remained in Hiva when he came to Easter Island with the party of *Hotu Matu'a.*

Marina Neru.   Daughter of *Lázaro Neru.* She was born in 1896 and is still living.

Maruata.   Son of *Kai Makoi,* one of the last ariki henua. With his father, he was taken to the Chincha Islands by Peruvians as a slave and died there.

Metoro.   An Easter Islander living in Tahiti. Bishop Tepano Jaussen recorded texts which he appeared to have read from rongorongo tablets.

Miru te Mata Nui.   Traditionally, the second son of *Hotu Matu'a.*

Moa Para.   Traditionally, a man who was magically carried to the Islet of Sala y Gómez by the akuaku Haua a Motu Motiro Hiva.

Moko Pinge'i.   Traditionally, the Hanau Momoko woman servant of a Hanau Eepe man, who betrayed the Hanau Eepe at the battle of Poike.

Ngaara.   One of the last ariki henua. He lived in the early nineteenth century.

Nuku Kehu.   Traditionally, the master builder of houses who came with the party of *Hotu Matu'a* and built the first house for the latter at Anakena.

Oroi.   Traditionally, the malevolent brother of *Hotu Matu'a.*

Ororoina.   According to tradition, a Hanau Eepe survivor of the battle of Poike. He later married a Hanau Momoko woman and had many descendants, some of whom still live on the island.

Paoa Hitaki.   An old islander, who in 1949 revealed to Juan Araki a rongorongo tablet concealed in a cave on the slopes of Rano Kau.

Pipi Horeko.   Traditionally, a man living at Maunga Toatoa, with whom *Ororoina* went to live after the battle of Poike.

Poie.   The leader of one of the opposing groups in a war that appears to have taken place between 1771 and 1773.

Rokoroko he Tau.   A member of the family of the ariki henua surviving at the time the missionaries arrived.

Teatea.   Traditionally, the father of *Vaka Tuku Onge.*

Teke.   Traditionally, the man in Hiva who stole from *Maeha* the yams that the party of *Hotu Matu'a* brought to Easter Island.

Tu'u ko Iho.   The ariki who traditionally commanded half of the double canoe of the party of *Hotu Matu'a.* Another ariki who lived in the second half of the eighteenth century had the same name.

Tu'u Maheke.   Traditionally, the eldest son of *Hotu Matu'a,* born at the time of his arrival on Easter Island.

Tu'u te Mata Nui.   Traditionally, a son of *Hotu Matu'a,* who at the time of the latter's death was given a district in the vicinity of Rano Kau.

Appendix I: People   165

Ure o Pea.   Traditionally, a grandson of *Ororoina.*

Ure Pooi.   A boy who figures in a tradition in which he tricks his sisters about their face paint.

Vakai a Heva.   Wife of *Hotu Matu'a,* who accompanied him to Easter Island from Hiva.

Vaka Tuku Onge.   Traditionally, a young man who lived near Mahatua and who was punished by akuaku for hunting birds in the territory of another group. His father was *Teatea.* Also the ancestral name of the family now bearing the name of Pate (see *José Pate).*

APPENDIX II. LIST OF ARIKI HENUA

The genealogical succession of ariki henua, or rulers, is much more confused on Easter Island than is the corresponding succession on many other Polynesian Islands. Four principal lists, which differ greatly from one another, have been published. The one collected by Alfred Métraux in 1934 includes thirty names and was regarded by Father Sebastian as the most reliable. On the basis of it he concluded that the first ariki henua, Hotu Matu'a, lived in the second half of the sixteenth century. This list follows, with the names in the forms recorded by Métraux, which are not always consistent with the forms used in the text.

1. Hotu matua
2. Tuu maheke
3. Miru
4. Ataranga
5. Ihu
6. Tuukunga te mamaru
7. Mahaki tapu vaeti
8. Nga uka te mahaki
9. Haumoana
10. Anakena
11. Tupa ariki
12. Marama
13. Tokoterangi
14. Kao aroaro
15. Mataivi
16. Kaohoto
17. Te Rahai
18. Te Ravarava
19. Te Hetuke
20. Tuu ko te mata nui
21. Hotu iti ko te mata iti
22. Honga
23. Takena
24. Tuukoihu
25. Kaimakoi
26. Ngaara
27. Ngaara rua
28. Kaimakoi iti
29. Rokoroko hetau
30. Rukunga

APPENDIX III. PLACES MENTIONED IN THE TEXT

The place names in this book are only a small fraction of those remembered on the island. Like all Polynesians, the Easter Islanders appear to have been obsessed with the idea of attaching names to even the most inconspicuous localities. Frequently these are associated with legends that serve to explain them. The map on pages 28-29 shows the location of all places mentioned.

Ahu Akapu. An ahu near the center of the west coast, from which, according to tradition, the establishment of each new ariki henua was proclaimed. A school for teaching the rongorongo script is said to have been located nearby.

Ahu Akivi. An ahu located inland of the center of the west coast. It was restored in 1960 and its seven statues were re-erected.

Ahu Ature Huke. An ahu at *Anakena*. Its single statue was re-erected in 1955 as a demonstration of local method.

Ahu Tahira. The best-known ahu at *Vinapu*. It is noteworthy for its unusually precisely dressed and fitted blocks, which are reminiscent of some central Andean masonry.

Ahu Te Pito Kura. An ahu on the north coast which has the largest statue ever transported to an ahu. The statue, called Paro, weighs about 82 tons.

Ahu Tongariki. An ahu at *Hotu Iti* on the south coast, one of the largest on the island, with fifteen large statues. It was completely destroyed by a tidal wave on May 22, 1960.

Ahu Vaiteka. A small ahu inland of the center of the west coast, related to

Ahu Akivi in an axis oriented to the rising sun at the equinox. It bears one small statue.

Akahanga.   A locality near the center of the south coast. Hotu Matu'a is traditionally said to have lived here for a time and to have been buried nearby.

Ana Kai Tangata.   A cave near the south end of the west coast, traditionally the site of cannibal feasts.

Anakena.   Today, the bay and the surrounding area near the center of the north coast where Hotu Matu'a is said to have made landfall. Originally the name designated only a cave where Hotu Matu'a is said to have lived until a house could be built for him. The old name of the bay is *Hanga Kaupari a Morie Roa.*

Ana More Mata Puku.   A cave on the eastern slope of *Poike*, in which specially selected young people of both sexes were secluded to protect their light skins from the effects of the sun.

Ana o Keke.   Another cave on the east coast of Poike which was used for the same purpose as *Ana More Mata Puku.*

Ariange.   Probably a locality in *Hiva.*

Hanga Hoonu.   A bay on the north coast; also called La Pérouse Bay.

Hanga Kaupari a Morie Roa.   Old name for the bay where Hotu Matu'a made his first landfall; see *Anakena.*

Hanga o Hiro.   A locality on the west side of the bay at *Anakena*, where traditionally was moored the half of the double canoe of the immigrant party of Hotu Matu'a commanded by Tu'u Ko Iho.

Hanga o Teo.   A bay at the west end of the north coast, formed of the remains of a volcanic crater invaded by the sea.

Hanga Roa.   A bay near the south end of the west coast; also called Cook's Bay.

Hangaroa.   The only village on the island occupied today; it is on the west coast.

Hanga Tangaroa Mea.   A small bay at *Hotu Iti* where the god Tangaroa is traditionally said to have been killed.

Hanga te Pau.   Bay at *Vinapu* near the west end of the south coast.

Hiro Moko.   A locality on the east side of the bay at *Anakena*, where traditionally was moored the half of the double canoe of the immigrant party of Hotu Matu'a commanded by him.

Hiva.   The place from which, according to tradition, Hotu Matu'a and his party came. Its location is unknown.

Hotu Iti.   Locality in the southeastern part of the island traditionally given by Hotu Matu'a to his youngest son Hotu Iti te Mata Iti.

Huareva.   A locality on the south coast between *Vaihu* and *Akahanga.*

Ko te Uhi a Ku'uku'u.   A locality on the slope of *Rano Kau* where traditionally

Ku'uku'u, one of the seven young men sent to make a reconnaissance of the island, planted a yam patch.

Mahatua. A district in the northeastern part of the island near the foot of *Poike.*

Maori. Traditionally, the part of *Hiva* where Hotu Matu'a lived before coming to Easter Island.

Marae Renga. Traditionally, the locality in *Maori* where Hotu Matu'a lived.

Mataveri. A district in the southwestern part of the island near the foot of *Rano Kau,* where the first part of the annual Manutara ceremonies was carried out; the ceremonies were continued at *Orongo.*

Maunga Orito. A hill near the west part of the south coast, noteworthy because it contains the largest deposit of obsidian on the island. It was much used as a source for materials for tools and weapons.

Maunga Terevaka. The volcano forming the northwest corner of the island. The highest elevation on the island, with a height of about 1,700 feet.

Maunga Toatoa. A small volcanic cone near the south coast.

Motu Iti. A small islet off the southwest corner of Easter Island.

Motu Kaokao. Another small islet off the southwest corner of the island.

Motu Nui. A small islet off the southwest coast of the island. It was to this islet that the hopu manu came in search of the first egg of the sooty tern as part of the annual ceremonies at *Orongo.*

Motu Motiro Hiva. See *Sala y Gómez.*

Motu Takataka. An islet located off the north shore of *Poike.*

Motu Toremo. An islet in *Hiva,* according to the tradition of the death of Hotu Matu'a.

Orongo. Ceremonial village on the edge of the crater of *Rano Kau* at the southwest corner of the island, which was the site of the second part of the annual manutara ceremonies.

Ovahe. A bay near the center of the north coast.

Poike. The volcano forming the east corner of the island. It is about 1,100 feet high.

Puha. A hill in the southwest part of the island.

Puko Puhipuhi. A locality near the north coast between *Hanga Hoonu* and *Taharoa,* where Uoke traditionally broke his lever.

Puku u'i Atua. A rock located inland of the central part of the west coast, near which, traditionally, lived a man whose wife was brought from *Hiva* by akuaku.

Punapau. A small natural water source located inland in the southwest part of the island. It lies near a small volcanic cone within which is located the quarry from which the red scoria topknots used on many statues on ahu were obtained. Today this name is usually applied to the quarry.

Rano Aroi.   The nearly dry fresh-water lake containing totora reeds, located in a satellite cone on the southern slope of *Maunga Terevaka.*

Rano Kau.   The largest fresh-water lake on the island. It is located in the crater of the volcano which forms the southwest corner of the island and has an extensive floating mat of totora reeds.

Rano Raraku.   The large fresh-water lake located inland near the east end of the south coast, within the crater of the volcano where the statue quarry is located; it contains an extensive growth of totora reeds.

Rapa Nui.   A name now widely used for Easter Island. It is said to have first been applied in the nineteenth century to distinguish this island from Rapa Iti located southeast of Tahiti.

Sala y Gómez.   Islet about 210 miles east-northeast of Easter Island, formerly called *Motu Motiro Hiva,* where, according to tradition, the akuaku Haua a Moto Motiro Hiva lived.

Taharoa.   A bay and locality located near the east end of the north coast.

Teapy.   A name for Easter Island given to Captain Cook. It has been little used since.

Te Hakarava.   A locality near the south coast at the foot of *Poike.*

Te Hue.   A locality on the west coast at the foot of *Rano Kau.*

Te Pito o te Henua.   "The navel of the world"; an old name for Easter Island. Pito (navel) carries the extended meaning of "center."

Te Umu o te Hanau Eepe.   "The earth oven of the Hanau Eepe." The trench at the foot of *Poike* extending from *Mahatua* to *Te Hakarava,* traditionally a fortification and the site of the great battle between the Hanau Eepe and the Hanau Momoko.

Tupo Tu'u.   Traditionally the first house occupied by Hotu Matu'a, said to have been built by the master builder Nuku Kehu. Some ruins survive at the site.

Vaihu.   A district on the south coast.

Vaitea.   A locality near the center of the island where the present-day sheep ranch and agricultural experiment station are located.

Vinapu.   A locality near the west end of the south coast, best known as the site of *Ahu Tahira.*

Whyhu.   A name for Easter Island given to Captain Cook. It almost certainly referred to the district of *Vaihu* and was mistakenly applied by Cook to the whole island.

REFERENCE NOTES

For complete bibliographical data, see Bibliography.

Chapter 1. TRADITIONS, RECORDS, AND GEOGRAPHY
1. Felipe Gonzales y Haedo, "Journals, Royal Commands, Minutes, and Despatches . . . ," in Bolton Glanville Corney (trans. and ed.), *The Voyage of Captain Don Felipe Gonzalez . . . to Easter Island in 1770-71*, p. 48.

Chapter 2. WHERE DID THE POLYNESIANS ORIGINATE?
1. Thor Heyerdahl, *Kon-Tiki*, p. 297

Chapter 3. MAN COMES TO EASTER ISLAND
1. Hyppolyte Roussel, "Ile de Pâques: Notice par le R.P. Hyppolyte Roussel, SS. CC. Apôtre de l'Ile Pâques" (sent to Valparaiso in 1869), *Annales des Sacrés-Coeurs*, no. 305, p. 360.

Chapter 4. BUILDING A NEW LIFE
1. Carl Friedrich Behrens, "Another Narrative of Jacob Roggeveen's Visit," in Bolton Glanville Corney (trans. and ed.), *The Voyage of Captain Don Felipe Gonzalez . . . to Easter Island in 1770-71*, p. 134.
2. Thor Heyerdahl, "The Prehistoric Culture of Easter Island," in Ichiro Yawata and Yosihiko H. Sinoto (eds.), *Prehistoric Culture in Oceania*, p. 134.

172

3. Jean François de Galaup de La Pérouse, *A Voyage Round the World in the Years 1785, 1786, 1787, and 1788*, p. 14.

4. Jacob Roggeveen, "Extract from the Official Log of Mr. Jacob Roggeveen Relating His Discovery of Easter Island," in Bolton Glanville Corney (trans. and ed.), *The Voyage of Captain Don Felipe Gonzalez . . . to Easter Island in 1770-71*, p. 13.

5. Behrens, "Another Narrative," pp. 134-135.

6. La Pérouse, A Voyage Round the World, p. 14.

Chapter 5. RELIGIOUS AND SOCIAL PRACTICES

1. Alfred Métraux, *Ethnology of Easter Island*, p. 314.

2. Francisco Antonio [?] Agüera y Infanzón, "Journal of the Occurrences During the Voyages of the Frigate Santa Rosalia from El Callao de Lima to the Island of David and thence to San Carlos de Chiloe in the Year 1770," in Bolton Glanville Corney (trans. and ed.), *The Voyage of Captain Don Felipe Gonzalez . . . to Easter Island in 1770-71*, p. 100.

3. Mrs. Scoresby Routledge, *The Mystery of Easter Island*, p. 236.

4. Behrens, "Another Narrative," p. 136.

5. Eugène Eyraud, "Lettre au T. R. P. Supèrieure Général de la Congréga-tion des Sacrés-Coeurs de Jésus et de Marie, Valparaiso, Decembre, 1864," *Annales de la Propagation de la Foi* (Lyon) vol. 38, 1866, p. 56.

6. Agüera, "Journal," pp. 96, 98.

7. *Ibid.*, p. 95.

Chapter 6. THE INSCRIBED TABLETS

1. Eyraud, "Lettre . . . 1864," p. 71.

2. Thomas Barthel, *Grundlagen zur Entzifferung der Osterinselschrift*, pp. 13-37.

3. Tepano Jaussen, "L'Ile de Pâques, Historíque et Ecriture," *Bulletin de Géographie Historíque et Descriptive* (Paris), No. 2, 1893, p. 252.

4. Guillaume de Hevesy, "Ecriture de l'Ile de Pâques," *Bulletin de la Société des Américanistes de Belgique* (Brussels), December 1932, pp. 120-127.

Chapter 7. THE DEATH OF HOTU MATU'A AND THE COMING OF OTHER IMMIGRANTS

1. William J. Thomson, "Te Pito Te Henua or Easter Island," *Report of the U.S. National Museum for the Year Ending June 30, 1889*, p. 534.

2. Roussel, "Ile de Pâques," p. 358.

3. Jaussen, "L'Ile de Pâques," p. 241.

4. Routledge, *Mystery of Easter Island*, p. 241.

5. Métraux, *Ethnology of Easter Island*, table 2.

6. Eyraud, "Lettre . . . 1864," p. 67.

7. Agüerra, "Journal," p. 109-110.

8. Peter H. Buck (Te Rangi Hiroa), *Vikings of the Sunrise*, p. 234.

9. Thor Heyerdahl, *American Indians in the Pacific*, p. 246.

Chapter 8. THE OUTDOOR ALTARS

1. Routledge, *Mystery of Easter Island*, p. 165.

2. *Ibid.*, p. 280.

3. William Mulloy, "The Ceremonial Center of Vinapu," in Thor Heyerdahl and Edwin Ferdon (eds.), *Archaeology of Easter Island*, p. 94.

4. Routledge, *Mystery of Easter Island*, p. 172.

Chapter 9. THE GREAT STATUES

1. Thor Heyerdahl, *Aku-Aku*, pp. 360-361.

2. Behrens, "Another Narrative," p. 133.

3. *Ibid.*, pp. 133-134.

4. Arne Skjölsvold, "The Stone Statues and Quarries of Rano Raraku," in Thor Heyerdahl and Edwin Ferdon (eds.), *Archaeology of Easter Island*, pp. 360-362.

5. Carlyle Smith, "A Temporal Sequence Derived from Certain Ahu," *ibid.*, p. 203.

6. *Ibid.*

Chapter 10. THE BEGINNING OF THE END

1. Carlyle Smith, "The Poike Ditch," in Thor Heyerdahl and Edwin Ferdon (eds.), *Archaeology of Easter Island*, p. 391.

2. Behrens, "Another Narrative," pp. 132-133.

Chapter 11. CONFLICT AND CANNIBALISM

1. Behrens, "Another Narrative," p. 134.

2. James Cook, *Second Voyage Towards the South Pole and Round the World . . . 1772-75*, pp. 276-296.

3. *Ibid.*, p. 281.

4. Otto von Kotzebue, *A Voyage of Discovery into the South Sea and Bering Straits*, p. 56.

5. Aubert du Petit-Thouars, *Voyage Autour du Monde sur la Frégate "La Venus" (1836-1839)*, vol. 2, p. 225.

6. Routledge, *Mystery of Easter Island*, p. 173.

7. Skjölsvold, "Stone Statues," p. 372.

8. Gonzalo Figueroa G-H and William Mulloy, "Medidas a Fin de Salvar el Tesoro Arqueológico de la Isla de Pascua," *Boletín de la Universidad de Chile*, no. 16, 1960, pp. 2-16; William Mulloy and Gonzalo Figueroa G-H, "Como fue Restaurado el Ahu Akivi en la Isla de Pascua," *ibid*, no. 27, 1963, pp. 4-11.

Chapter 12. FINAL TRAGEDY

1. Roussel, "Ile de Pâques," p. 423.

2. Kotzebue, *Voyage of Discovery*, pp. 56-57; J. A. Moernhout, *Voyage aux Iles du Grand Océan*, vol. 2, pp. 276-278.

3. Moernhout, *Voyage*, vol. 2, pp. 278-279.

4. Routledge, *Mystery of Easter Island*, pp. 205-206; Pacôme Olivier, "Lettre du R.P. Pacôme Olivier, Vice-Provencial de la Congrégation des Sacrés-Coeurs de Jésus de Marie á Valparaiso au T.R.P. Supérieur Général de la Même Congrégation á Paris. Dec. 1864," *Annales de la Association de la Propagation de la Foi* (Lyon), vol. 38, 1869, p. 50; T. de Lapelin, "L'Ile de Pâques," *Revue Maritime et Coloniale* (Paris), vol. 35, 1872, pp. 543-544; Jaussen, "L'Ile de Pâques," p. 242; W. A. Powell, "Detailed Report upon Easter Island or Rapa-nui," *Proceedings of the Royal Geographical Society of Australia*, vol. 3, p. 141.

GLOSSARY

In the Easter Island language, nouns have the same form in both singular and plural.

ahu.   A large outdoor altar, variant of a kind widely known in Polynesia as *marae.* On Easter Island the word ahu is applied to structures of several kinds. *Ahu moai* are large outdoor altars bearing statues and sometimes secondarily used for burial. A few included in this group are without statues but architecturally similar. Rectangular ahu are large, rubble-filled, masonry platforms containing tombs. *Ahu poepoe* are similar but elevated at one or both ends. Semipyramidal ahu have the form of low, much elongated pyramids. They are of rubble-filled masonry and contain tombs. *Avanga,* which are platforms of various types bearing or containng tombs or crematory cysts, are sometimes considered to be ahu, and the term *ahu avanga* is heard occasionally.

akuaku.   A supernatural being, Akuaku are usually thought of as malevolent, but typically they appear to have been friendly to their own kinsmen while hostile to others, and some appear to have been benevolent to all.

ana.   Cave. The word is sometimes applied to artificial cavelike structures of masonry.

ao.   A long wooden baton in the form of a club. It appears to have been a symbol of command.

ariki.   An individual of high rank. Ariki possessed impersonal supernatural power called *mana* which they used to benefit the community, and to enforce prohibitions.

ariki henua. The supreme religious leader and symbol of the island. He lived in isolation and did not exercise political power, though his *mana* was important to the community.

aringa ora. "Living faces"; a name applied to the large statues.

Atamu. Adam. The old form of the present-day family name *Atan*. The word was learned from missionaries.

Atan. See *Atamu*.

aue. An exclamation of despair or wonder used on Easter Island and widely in Polynesia.

avanga. Platform bearing or containing tombs or crematory cysts; see *ahu*.

eepe. Stocky or heavy-set; has been erroneously translated as "long-eared."

epe. Earlobe.

epe roroa. Elongated earlobe.

haka no nonga. Named fishing grounds around Easter Island. The names of fifteen such areas are remembered.

Hanau Eepe. A kin-group traditionally said to have arrived at Easter Island after Hotu Matu'a. The name, frequently erroneously translated as "long ears," means "stocky or heavy-set people."

Hanau Momoko. The kin-groups who came with Hotu Matu'a or developed from the descendants of these. The name, frequently erroneously translated as "short ears," means "slender people."

hanga. Bay.

haoa. Wound.

Haoa. A present-day family name.

hare. House.

hare moa. Chicken house.

hare paenga. One form of early dwelling. Its thatched superstructure was shaped like an overturned canoe, and its foundation was made of precisely dressed and fitted large basalt blocks. Holes in these received the vertical members of the superstructure. Such house foundations are frequently seen inland of the ahu in rows or groups and are traditionally said to have been occupied by the priesthoods. The house traditionally first occupied by Hotu Matu'a was of this type.

hatuke. Name of one kind of yam traditionally said to have been stolen from Hiva.

hau. Hibiscus (*Triumfetta semitriloba*). Its bark produced fiber used to make cordage.

ha'u. Hat.

ha'u moai. Red scoria topknots placed on many statues on *ahu*.

ha'u teketeke. A feather hat with two long plumes in front. It was worn backward to indicate displeasure.

Haua a Motu Motiro Hiva. An *akuaku* traditionally said to have lived on the islet of Sala y Gómez about 210 miles northeast of Easter Island.

Hikinga kaunga. Dances in which *poki huru hare* (children who had been kept from exposure to the sun) were exhibited to display the beauty of their light skins.

Hiro. A widely known Polynesian god who may once have been worshipped on Easter Island. His name survives in an old chant and in place names.

hopu manu. Specially trained athletes who during the September ceremonies at Orongo swam to *Motu Nui* and competed to bring back the first egg of the *manutara*. The sponsor of the winning hopu manu became the *tangata manu* for the following year.

huru hare. Inside the house.

inaki. Vegetable food used to accompany fish, fowl, or meat at meals.

iti. small.

iuhi tatu. Slender bone needle with three or four points, used as a tattooing instrument.

kahi. Tuna fish.

kai. Eat.

kakau. Weapon consisting of a large obsidian blade *(mataa)* attached to a short handle for hand-to-hand combat.

kekepu. Unknown animal remembered in traditions as having been used for food in Hiva. It may have been the pig.

kena. A marine bird. Kind unknown.

kiea. Red pigment found on the slopes of Poike and used for painting faces, bodies, clothing and other things.

kio. Refugees who hid in caves from enemies.

kio'e. Polynesian rat (probably *Rattus concolor* or *Mus maori*), used for food. It now appears to be extinct and has been replaced by introduced species.

ko hau ika. Rongorongo tablets bearing texts dedicated to the memory of people who fell in wars or other conflicts.

ko hau kiri taku ki te atua. Rongorongo tablets bearing texts recording religious hymns in honor of *Makemake* and other divine personalities.

ko hau motu mo rongorongo. Lines of script for recitation; the full name of the wooden tablets bearing script.

ko hau rongorongo. Lines for recitation. Shortened form of name for wooden tablets bearing script.

ko hau ta'u. Rongorongo tablets bearing records of crimes or other deeds of individuals.

koro. Ceremonies celebrated with a series of songs and feasting. They were apparently given in honor of a deceased person or in memory of an important event. There were many kinds.

Kuaha. An *akuaku* whose name appears in the tradition of the death of Hotu Matu'a. He may have lived in Hiva. See also *Kuihi, Opakake, Tongau.*

Kuihi. Another *akuaku* whose name appears in the tradition of the death of Hotu Matu'a. He also may have lived in Hiva.

kumara. Sweet potato *(Ipomoea batatas).*

mahute. Paper mulberry *(Broussonetia papyrifera).* The bark was beaten to make cloth similar to the *tapa* of other parts of Polynesia. The word also applied to the finished bark cloth.

Makemake. The creator and most important god on Easter Island. This name is not known from other islands. He may be a counterpart of a god known widely elsewhere as *Tane.*

makohe. Marine bird of dark plumage.

makoi nau opata. Sandalwood tree *(Thespesia populnea).* The nuts of this tree are traditionally said to have been the only vegetable food available to Hotu Matu'a's party when they first arrived on the island.

mana. Impersonal supernatural power possessed by the *ariki* and used to enforce prohibitions of *tapu* and to benefit the community.

manavai. Small argricultural enclosure surrounded by masonry walls or excavated into the ground and lined with masonry walls. These are frequently seen today in large clusters near the old domestic establishments. They provided protection from wind.

manutara. The sooty tern. This bird and its eggs figured in the cult of the *Tangata manu* and in the ceremonies carried out each year at Orongo.

maori. Honorific title used by masters of any craft.

maori anga moai. Master sculptor.

maori ko hau rongorongo. Priests skilled in the art of reading and writing the *rongorongo* script.

marae. A widely used Polynesian word for large outdoor altars of the type called *ahu* on Easter Island.

mare. Asthma. Thought to be a punishment for violation of the *tapu* against eating tuna and other large fish between approximately May and September.

mata. Eye; kin-group.

mataa. Large, usually irregularly leaf-shaped, percussion-flaked obsidian blades used as spear points, knives, and for other purposes.

mataa ko hou. A *mataa* attached to a long shaft and used as a throwing spear.

matatoa. War leader.

mata'u. Instructor who taught young men the arts of war.

maunga. Mountain.

miro. Wood; by extension, boat.

miro oone. Boat of earth. An elongated mound of earth in the form of a boat. In one kind of *koro* ceremony the participants assembled on the mound to represent a boat crew.

Miti. A corruption of the English title Mister.

moa. Chicken.

Moaha. An ancestral spirit.

moai. Statue. Applied without qualification to the large stone statues, and with qualifiers to other kinds of statues, as *moai kavakava.*

moai kavakava. Statue with ribs; a wooden figure in the form of a desiccated corpse. Said first to have been carved by the *ariki* called Tu'u ko Iho, who exhibited such figures as puppets. These figures are said to represent *akuaku.*

moki oone. Sandalwood nuts (*Thespesia populnea*).

moko. Lizard. There are two varieties of small lizard (*Ablepharus boutonii* and *Lepidodactylus lugubris*) on the island. A local wood-carving motif of what appears to be a somewhat anthropomorphized lizard is also called *moko.*

motu. Islet.

neru. Specially selected young people of both sexes who were secluded in two caves on Poike, Ana o Keke and Ana More Mata Puku, to protect their light skins from the sun.

niuhi tapaka'i. A fish, probably the hammerhead shark.

niu. Coconut.

nui. Large.

o'oa take heuheu. Onomatopoeic for the crowing of a rooster.

Opakake. An *akuaku* whose name appears in the tradition of the death of Hotu Matu'a. He may have lived in Hiva.

orro, orro, orro. Cry of a *Hanau Eepe* warrior when pricked by the spears of the *Hanau Momoko* at the Poike battle. Traditionally said to have attracted the attention of the Hanau Momoko because the double "r" sound did not occur in their language. An item of evidence offered to suggest that the language of the Hanau Eepe was different from that of the Hanau Momoko.

Oteka. Traditionally, the name of the half of the double canoe in which Hotu Matu'a arrived on the island.

Oua. Traditionally, the name of the half of the double canoe of Hotu Matu'a's party in which the *ariki* Tu'u ko Iho arrived.

paina. One kind of *koro* ceremony traditionally said to have been given by a son to honor his dead father and a friend of the latter. It involved building on the plaza of an *ahu* a conical, hollow structure with an open-mouthed head at the top. The son spoke a eulogy from inside the head.

pakia. Sea lion.

pakia re'o-o. "Lying sea lion"; reference to the god *Tangaroa* who was killed in the form of a sea lion.

paoa. The wooden club used in war; by extension, a warrior.

Paoa. A present-day family name.

Paro. Traditionally, the name of the single statue at Ahu te Pito Kura. It weighs about 82 tons and is the largest to have been transported to an *ahu*.

paroko. Small fish of unknown kind.

Pate. A present-day family name.

pipi horeko. A small cairn traditionally said to have been used as a boundary marker. Sometimes these contain burials.

poki. Child or children.

poki huru hare. "Children inside the house"; specially selected children who were kept indoors to preserve the light color of their skins. They were exhibited in dances called *hikinga kaunga*.

Rangi. Probably a corruption of an unknown English name.

rano. A crater lake; today used by extension for the crater in which the lake lies.

Rapahango. An *akuaku* of unusually benevolent disposition, companion of *Tare*. Also a present-day family name.

re'e. Raw.

reimiro. A crescent-shaped pectoral of wood worn by *ariki*.

riu. A kind of festival involving group singing.

roa. Long.

rongorongo. Recitation; the script of the island.

Tane. A god widely worshipped in Polynesia. This name is not known to occur on Easter Island. The island god *Makemake* may be a counterpart of Tane.

tangata. Man, men, people.

tangata heuheu henua. Farmer.

tangata hiva. Foreigner.

tangata honui. Man of rank; leader of a kin-group.

tangata manu. Bird man. The individual who, as a result of the success of his *hopu manu* in returning to Orongo with the first egg of the *manutara* during the annual ceremonies there, held for one year a special ceremonial position which gave his group considerable power.

tangata paoa. Warrior below the rank of *matatoa*, frequently shortened to *paoa*.

tangata rara haoa. An individual skilled in the curing of wounds.

tangata rima toto. Man with bloody hands. Name applied to the *matatoa*.

tangata tere vaka. Fisherman.

Tangaroa. A widely known Polynesian god traditionally said to have been killed on Easter Island.

tapa. Bark cloth. A common Polynesian word, not used on Easter Island.

tapu. A prohibition enforced by the impersonal supernatural power called *mana*.

Tare. An *akuaku* of unusually benevolent disposition; *Rapahango* was his companion.

taro (Colocasia antiquorum). A large, white, edible tuber grown by the islanders in dry fields.

Tauto. Name of a statue traditionally left behind in Hiva at the time of the immigration of Hotu Matu'a; he is said to have sent back a special expedition to obtain it and other statues.

ti (Cordyline terminalis). A small plant with very sweet roots, cultivated and used for food.

toki. Adze of stone.

Tongau. An *akuaku* whose name appears in the tradition of the death of Hotu Matu'a. He may have lived in Hiva.

totora (Scirpus riparius). A reed, used for a variety of purposes, which grows in the crater lakes Rano Aroi, Rano Raraku, and Rano Kau. This word does not appear to be of local origin, though it is now widely used.

tuku riu. The special kneeling posture of singers at *riu* festivals.

tuku turi. Kneeling posture. Sometimes shortened to *tuku*.

tumu ivi atua. Priests who took part in the *manutara* ceremonies and performed other functions.

tu'ura. Servants of the *ariki*.

uhi. Yam *(Dioscorea* species).

umu. Earth oven in which food was cooked by means of hot stones.

umu tahu. Earth oven prepared for ritual purposes; also the food prepared in such an oven.

Uoke. A supernatural being who traditionally traveled about the Pacific destroying islands with a gigantic lever; he is said to have broken his lever at Easter Island and thus been unable to destroy it.

vaka ivi. "Boat of bones"; name applied to a kind of tomb.

BIBLIOGRAPHY

WORKS BY SEBASTIAN ENGLERT

Diccionario Rapanui-Español. Santiago de Chile: Prensas de la Universidad de Chile, 1938.

Tradiciones de la Isla de Pascua. Santiago de Chile: Publicaciones de la Comisión de Estudios sobre la Isla de Pascua, Universidad de Chile, 1939.

La Tierra de Hotu Matu'a. Santiago de Chile: Imprenta y Editorial "San Francisco," 1948.

Primer Siglo Cristiano de la Isla de Pascua. Santiago de Chile: Escuela Lito-Tipografica Salesiana "La Gratitud Nacional," 1964.

"Easter Island and Its First Century of Christ," *Worldmission*, vol. 16, no. 1, Spring, 1965, pp. 40-45.

WORKS CITED

Agüera y Infanzón, Francisco Antonio [?]. "Journal of the Occurrences During the Voyage of the Frigate Santa Rosalia from El Callao de Lima to the Island of David and thence to San Carlos de Chiloe in the Year 1770" in Corney, *The Voyage of Captain Don Felipe Gonzalez*, pp. 83-111. See Corney.

Barthel, Thomas. *Grundlagen zur Entzifferung der Osterinselschrift.* Hamburg: Cram, De Gruyter and Company, 1958.

Behrens, Carl Friederich. "Another Narrative of Jacob Roggeveen's Visit Translated by the Editor from the German of Carl Friederich Behrens: Der wohlversüchte Südländer, das ist: ausfürliche Reise-Beschreibung um die

Welt," in Corney, *The Voyage of Captain Don Felipe Gonzalez*, pp. 131-137.

See Corney.

Buck, Peter H. (Te Rangi Hiroa). *Vikings of the Sunrise.* Philadelphia: Lippincott, 1938.

Cook, James. *Second Voyage Towards the South Pole and Round the World Performed in the "Resolution" and "Adventure," 1772-75.* 2 vols. London: W. Strahan and T. Cadell, 1777.

Corney, Bolton Glanville (trans. and ed.). *The Voyage of Captain Don Felipe Gonzalez in the Ship of the Line San Lorenzo with the Frigate Santa Rosalia in Company to Easter Island in 1770-71.* Cambridge: The Hakluyt Society, Issued for 1903, 1908.

Includes the accounts of Agüera y Infanzon; Behrens, Gonzalez y Haedo; Roggeveen; see individual entries.

Croft, Thomas. "Letter of April 30th, 1874, from Thomas Croft, Papeete, Tahiti, to the President of the California Academy of Sciences," *Proceedings of the California Academy of Sciences,* vol. 5, 1875, pp. 317-323.

Eyraud, Eugène. "Lettre au T. R. P. Supérieur Général de la Congrégation des Sacrés-Coeurs de Jésus et de Marie—Valparaiso, Décembre, 1864," *Annales de la Association de la Propagation de la Foi* (Lyon), vol. 38, 1866, pp. 52-71, 124-138.

Figueroa G-H, Gonzalo, and Mulloy, William. "Medidas a Fin de Salvar el Tesoro Arqueológico de la Isla de Pascua," *Boletín de la Universidad de Chile* (Santiago de Chile), no. 14, 1960, pp. 2-16.

Gonzalez y Haedo, Felipe. "Journals, Royal Commands, Minutes, and Despatches (with enclosures) relating to the Voyage of the Ship of the Line San Lorenzo and her Consort the Frigate Santa Rosalia in the Years 1770-71 in Search of Easter Island," in Corney, *The Voyage of Captain Don Felipe Gonzalez*, pp. 27-159.

See Corney.

Hevesy, Guillaume de. "Ecriture de l'Ile de Pâques," *Bulletin de la Société des Américanistes de Belgique* (Brussels), Décembre, 1932, pp. 120-127.

Heyerdahl, Thor. *Kon-Tiki.* Chicago: Rand McNally, 1950.

———*American Indians in the Pacific.* Chicago: Rand McNally, 1952.

———*Aku-Aku.* Chicago: Rand McNally, 1958.

———"The Prehistoric Culture of Easter Island," in *Prehistoric Culture in Oceania.* Ichiro Yawata and Yosihiko H. Sinoto, (eds.) Honolulu: Bishop Museum Press, 1968. pp. 133-140.

Heyerdahl, Thor, and Skjölsvold, Arne. *Archaelogical Evidence of Pre-Spanish Visits to the Galapagos Islands*. Memoirs of the Society for American Archaeology, vol. 22, no. 2, part 3. Salt Lake City: The Society for American Archaeology, 1956.

Heyerdahl, Thor, and Ferdon, Edwin (eds.). *Archaeology of Easter Island*. Monographs of the School of American Research and the Museum of New Mexico, no. 24, part 1. Stockholm: Forum Publishing House, 1961.
Includes Mulloy, "The Ceremonial Center of Vinapu"; Skjölsvold, "The Stone Statues and Quarries of Rano Raraku"; Smith, "A Temporal Sequence Derived from Certain Ahu" and "The Poike Ditch"; see individual entries.

Jaussen, Tepano. "L'Ile de Pâques, Historique et Ecriture," *Bulletin de Géographie Historique et Descriptive* (Paris), No. 2, 1893, pp. 240-270.

Kotzebue, Otto von. *A Voyage of Discovery into the South Sea and Bering Straits*. 3 vols. London, 1821.

Lapelin, T. de. "L'Ile de Pâques." *Revue Maritime et Coloniale* (Paris), vol. 35, 1872.

La Pérouse, Jean François de Galaup de. *A Voyage Round the World in the Years 1785, 1786, 1787, and 1788*. Edited by M. L. A. Milet-Mureau. 3 vols. Paris, 1791. Translated to English and published in London in 1798 by J. Johnson.

Lavachery, Henri. *Les Pétroglyphes de l'Ile de Pâques*. Antwerp: De Sikel, Kruishofstraat, 1939.

Metraux, Alfred. *Ethnology of Easter Island*. Bulletin 160, Bernice P. Bishop Museum. Honolulu, 1940.

Moernhout, J. A. *Voyages aux Iles du Grand Océan*. 2 vols. Paris, 1837.

Mulloy, William. "The Ceremonial Center of Vinapu," in Heyerdahl and Ferdon, *Archaeology of Easter Island*, pp. 92-167.
See Heyerdahl and Ferdon.

Mulloy, William, and Figueroa G-H, Gonzalo. "Como fue Restaurado el Ahu Akiva en la Isla de Pascua," *Boletín de la Universidad de Chile* (Santiago de Chile), No. 27, 1963, pp. 4-11.

Olivier, Pacôme. "Lettre du R. P. Pacôme Olivier, Vice-Provencial de la Congrégation des Sacrés-Coeurs de Jésus et de Marie a Valparaiso au T. R. P. Supérieur Général de la même Congrégation a Paris. Dec. 1864", *Annales de la Association de la Propagation de la Foi* (Lyon), vol. 38, 1866, pp. 44-52.

Petit-Thouars, Aubert du. *Voyage autour du Monde sur la Frégate "La Venus" (1836-1839)*. 4 vols. Paris, 1841.

Powell, W. A. "Detailed Report upon Easter Island or Rapa-nui," *Proceedings of the Royal Geographical Society of Australia* (Adelaide), vol. 3, 1899, pp. 138-142.

Roggeveen, Jacob. "Extract from the Official Log of Mr. Jacob Roggeveen Relating to His Discovery of Easter Island," in Corney, *The Voyage of Captain Don Felipe Gonzalez*, pp. 1-24.
See Corney.

Roussel, Hyppolyte. "Ile de Pâques. Notice par le R. P. Hyppolyte Roussel, SS. CC. Apôtre de l'Ile Pâques" (sent to Valparaiso in 1869), *Annales des Sacrés-Coeurs* (Paris), 1926, no. 305, pp. 355-360; no. 307, pp. 423-430; no. 308, pp. 462-466; no. 309, pp. 495-499.

Routledge, Mrs. Scoresby. *The Mystery of Easter Island.* London: Sifton Praed, 1919.

Skjölsvold, Arne. "The Stone Statues and Quarries of Rano Raraku," in Heyerdahl and Ferdon; *Archaeolgy of Easter Island*, pp. 339-379.
See Heyerdahl and Ferdon.

Smith, Carlyle. "A Temporal Sequence Derived from Certain Ahu," *ibid.*, pp. 181-219.
————"The Poike Ditch," *ibid.*, pp. 385-391.

Thomson, William J. "Te Pito Te Henua or Easter Island," *Report of the U. S. National Museum for the Year Ending June 30, 1889*, pp. 447-552. Washington: U. S. Government Printing Office, 1889.

INDEX

warriors, 137-38, 140
water, scarcity, 84
weapons, 139-40
wood, 60

writing, 77
    teaching, 77

yams, 53, 54-55